W9-CZR-387

Programming Elastic MapReduce

Kevin Schmidt and Christopher Phillips

Beijing · Cambridge · Farnham · Köln · Sebastopol · Tokyo

Programming Elastic MapReduce

by Kevin Schmidt and Christopher Phillips

Copyright © 2014 Kevin Schmidt and Christopher Phillips. All rights reserved.

Printed in the United States of America.

Published by O'Reilly Media, Inc., 1005 Gravenstein Highway North, Sebastopol, CA 95472.

O'Reilly books may be purchased for educational, business, or sales promotional use. Online editions are also available for most titles (*http://my.safaribooksonline.com*). For more information, contact our corporate/institutional sales department: 800-998-9938 or *corporate@oreilly.com*.

Editors: Mike Loukides and Courtney Nash	**Indexer:** Judith McConville
Production Editor: Christopher Hearse	**Cover Designer:** Randy Comer
Copyeditor: Kim Cofer	**Interior Designer:** David Futato
Proofreader: Rachel Monaghan	**Illustrator:** Rebecca Demarest

December 2013:   First Edition

Revision History for the First Edition:

2013-12-09:   First release

See *http://oreilly.com/catalog/errata.csp?isbn=9781449363628* for release details.

Nutshell Handbook, the Nutshell Handbook logo, and the O'Reilly logo are registered trademarks of O'Reilly Media, Inc. *Programming Elastic MapReduce*, the cover image of an eastern kingsnake, and related trade dress are trademarks of O'Reilly Media, Inc.

Many of the designations used by manufacturers and sellers to distinguish their products are claimed as trademarks. Where those designations appear in this book, and O'Reilly Media, Inc., was aware of a trademark claim, the designations have been printed in caps or initial caps.

While every precaution has been taken in the preparation of this book, the publisher and authors assume no responsibility for errors or omissions, or for damages resulting from the use of the information contained herein.

ISBN: 978-1-449-36362-8

[LSI]

Table of Contents

Preface

Many organizations have a treasure trove of data stored away in the many silos of information within them. To unlock this information and use it to compete in the marketplace, organizations have begun looking to Hadoop and "Big Data" as the key to gaining an advantage over their competition. Many organizations, however, lack the knowledgeable resources and data center space to launch large-scale Hadoop solutions for their data analysis projects.

Amazon Elastic MapReduce (EMR) is Amazon's Hadoop solution, running in Amazon's data center. Amazon's solution is allowing organizations to focus on the data analysis problems they want to solve without the need to plan data center buildouts and maintain large clusters of machines. Amazon's pay-as-you-go model is just another benefit that allows organizations to start these projects with no upfront costs and scale instantly as the project grows. We hope this book inspires you to explore Amazon Web Services (AWS) and Amazon EMR, and to use this book to help you launch your next great project with the power of Amazon's cloud to solve your biggest data analysis problems.

This book focuses on the core Amazon technologies needed to build an application using AWS and EMR. We chose an application to analyze log data as our case study throughout this book to demonstrate the power of EMR. Log analysis is a good case study for many data analysis problems that organizations faced. Computer logfiles contain large amounts of diverse data from different sources and can be mined to gain valuable intelligence. More importantly, logfiles are ubiquitous across computer systems and provide a ready and available data set with which you can start solving data analysis problems.

Here is an outline of what this book provides:

- Sample configurations for third-party software
- Step-by-step configurations for AWS
- Sample code

- Best practices
- Gotchas

The intent is not to provide a book that has all the code, configuration, and so on, to be able to plop this application on AWS and start going. Instead, we will provide guidance to help you see how to put together a system or application in a cloud environment and describe core issues you may face in working within AWS in building your own project.

You will get the most out of this book if you have a some experience developing or managing applications developed for the traditional data center, but now want to learn how you can move your applications and data into a cloud environment. You should be comfortable using development toolsets and reviewing code samples, architecture diagrams, and configuration examples to understand basic concepts covered in this book. We will use the command line and command-line tools in Unix on a number of the examples we present, so it would not hurt to be familiar with navigating the command line and using basic Unix command-line utilities. The examples in this book can be used on Windows systems too, but you may need to load third-party utilities like Cygwin (*http://www.cygwin.com/*) to follow along.

This book will challenge you with new ways of looking at your applications outside of your traditional data center walls, but hopefully it will open your eyes to the possibilities of what you can accomplish when you focus on the problems you are trying to solve rather than the many administrative issues of building out new servers in a private data center.

What Is AWS?

Amazon Web Services (*http://aws.amazon.com/what-is-aws/*) is the name of the computing platform started by Amazon in 2006. AWS offers a suite of services to companies and third-party developers to build solutions using the computing and software resources hosted in Amazon's data centers around the globe. Amazon Elastic MapReduce (*http://aws.amazon.com/elasticmapreduce/*) is one of many available AWS services. Developers and companies only pay for the resources they use with a pay-as-you-go model in AWS. This model is changing the approach many businesses take at looking at new projects and initiatives. New initiatives can get started and scale within AWS as they build a customer base and grow without much of the usual upfront costs of buying new servers and infrastructure. Using AWS, companies can now focus on innovation and on building great solutions. They are able to focus less on building and maintaining data centers and the physical infrastructure and can focus on developing solutions.

What's in This Book?

This book is organized as follows. Chapter 1 introduces cloud computing and helps you understand Amazon Web Service and Amazon Elastic MapReduce. Chapter 2 gets us started exploring the Amazon tools we will be using to examine log data and execute our first Job Flow inside of Amazon EMR. In Chapter 3, we get down to the business of exploring the types of analyses that can be done with Amazon EMR using a number of MapReduce design patterns, and review the results we can get out of log data. In Chapter 5, we delve into machine learning techniques and how these can be implemented and utilized in our application to build intelligent systems that can take action or recommend a solution to a problem. Finally, in Chapter 6, we review project cost estimation for AWS and EMR applications and how to perform cost analysis of a project.

Sign Up for AWS

To get started, you need to sign up for AWS. If you are already an AWS user, you can skip this section because you already have access to each of the AWS services used throughout this book. If you are a new user, we will get you started in this section.

To sign up for AWS, go to the AWS website (*http://aws.amazon.com/what-is-aws/*), as shown in Figure P-1.

Figure P-1. Amazon Web Services home page

You will need to provide a phone number to verify that you are setting up a valid account and you will also need to provide a credit card number to allow Amazon to bill you for the usage of AWS services. We will cover how to estimate, review, and set up billing alerts within AWS in Chapter 6.

After signing up for an AWS account, go to your My Account page to review the services to which you now have access. Figure P-2 shows the available services under our account, but your results will likely look somewhat different.

> Remember, there are charges associated with the use of AWS, and a number of the examples and exercises in this book will incur charges to your account. With a new AWS account, there is a free tier (*http:// aws.amazon.com/free/*). To minimize the costs while learning about Amazon Elastic MapReduce, review the free-tier limitations, turn off instances after running through your exercises, and learn how to estimate costs in Chapter 6.

Figure P-2. AWS services available after signup

Code Samples in This Book

There are numerous code samples and examples throughout this book. Many of the examples are built using the Java programming language or Hadoop Java libraries. To get the most out of this book and follow along, you need to have a system set up to do Java development and Hadoop Java JAR files to build an application that Amazon EMR can consume and execute. To get ready to develop and build your next application, review Appendix C to set up your development environment. This is not a requirement, but it will help you get the most value out of the material presented in the chapters.

Conventions Used in This Book

The following typographical conventions are used in this book:

Italic
> Indicates new terms, URLs, email addresses, filenames, and file extensions.

`Constant width`
> Used for program listings, as well as within paragraphs to refer to program elements such as variable or function names, databases, data types, environment variables, statements, and keywords.

Constant width bold

Shows commands or other text that should be typed literally by the user.

Constant width italic

Shows text that should be replaced with user-supplied values or by values determined by context.

 This icon signifies a tip, suggestion, or general note.

 This icon indicates a warning or caution.

Using Code Examples

This book is here to help you get your job done. In general, if example code is offered with this book, you may use it in your programs and documentation. You do not need to contact us for permission unless you're reproducing a significant portion of the code. For example, writing a program that uses several chunks of code from this book does not require permission. Selling or distributing a CD-ROM of examples from O'Reilly books does require permission. Answering a question by citing this book and quoting example code does not require permission. Incorporating a significant amount of example code from this book into your product's documentation does require permission.

We appreciate, but do not require, attribution. An attribution usually includes the title, author, publisher, and ISBN. For example: "*Programming Elastic MapReduce* by Kevin J. Schmidt and Christopher Phillips (O'Reilly). Copyright 2014 Kevin Schmidt and Christopher Phillips, 978-1-449-36362-8."

If you feel your use of code examples falls outside fair use or the permission given above, feel free to contact us at *permissions@oreilly.com*.

Safari® Books Online

 *Safari Books Online* is an on-demand digital library that delivers expert content in both book and video form from the world's leading authors in technology and business.

Technology professionals, software developers, web designers, and business and creative professionals use Safari Books Online as their primary resource for research, problem solving, learning, and certification training.

Safari Books Online offers a range of product mixes and pricing programs for organizations, government agencies, and individuals. Subscribers have access to thousands of books, training videos, and prepublication manuscripts in one fully searchable database from publishers like O'Reilly Media, Prentice Hall Professional, Addison-Wesley Professional, Microsoft Press, Sams, Que, Peachpit Press, Focal Press, Cisco Press, John Wiley & Sons, Syngress, Morgan Kaufmann, IBM Redbooks, Packt, Adobe Press, FT Press, Apress, Manning, New Riders, McGraw-Hill, Jones & Bartlett, Course Technology, and dozens more. For more information about Safari Books Online, please visit us online.

How to Contact Us

Please address comments and questions concerning this book to the publisher:

O'Reilly Media, Inc.
1005 Gravenstein Highway North
Sebastopol, CA 95472
800-998-9938 (in the United States or Canada)
707-829-0515 (international or local)
707-829-0104 (fax)

We have a web page for this book, where we list errata, examples, and any additional information. You can access this page at *http://oreil.ly/Prog-Elastic-MapReduce*.

To comment or ask technical questions about this book, send email to *bookquestions@oreilly.com*.

For more information about our books, courses, conferences, and news, see our website at *http://www.oreilly.com*.

Find us on Facebook: *http://facebook.com/oreilly*

Follow us on Twitter: *http://twitter.com/oreillymedia*

Watch us on YouTube: *http://www.youtube.com/oreillymedia*

lost, you lose the work in progress by the master *and* the core and task nodes to which it had delegated work.

Core group instance

Core group instance members run the map and reduce portions of our Job Flow, and store intermediate data to the Hadoop Distributed File System (HDFS) storage in our Amazon EMR cluster. The master node manages the tasks and data delegated to the core and task nodes. Due to the HDFS storage aspects of core nodes, a loss of a core node will result in data loss and possible failure of the complete Job Flow.

Task group instance

The task group is optional. It can do some of the dirty computational work of the map and reduce jobs, but does not have HDFS storage of the data and intermediate results. The lack of HDFS storage on these instances means the data needs to be transferred to these nodes by the master for the task group to do the work in the Job Flow.

The master and core group instances are critical components in the Amazon EMR cluster. A loss of a node in the master or core group instance can cause an application to fail and need to be restarted. Task groups are optional because they do not control a critical function of the Amazon EMR cluster. In terms of jobs and responsibilities, the master group must maintain the status of tasks. A loss of a node in the master group may make it so the status of a running task cannot be determined or retrieved and lead to Job Flow failure.

The core group runs tasks and maintains the data retained in the Amazon EMR cluster. A loss of a core group node may cause data loss and Job Flow failure.

A task node is only responsible for running tasks delegated to it from the master group and utilizes data maintained by the core group. A failure of a task node will lose any interim calculations. The master node will retry the task node when it detects failure in the running job. Because task group nodes do not control the state of jobs or maintain data in the Amazon EMR cluster, task nodes are optional, but they are one of the key areas where capacity of the Amazon EMR cluster can be expanded or shrunk without affecting the stability of the cluster.

Amazon EMR and the Hadoop Ecosystem

As we've already seen, Amazon EMR uses Hadoop and its MapReduce framework at its core. Accordingly, many of the other core Apache Software Foundation projects that work with Hadoop also work with Amazon EMR. There are also many other AWS services that may be useful when you're running and monitoring Amazon EMR applications. Some of these will be covered briefly in this book:

Safari Books Online offers a range of product mixes and pricing programs for organizations, government agencies, and individuals. Subscribers have access to thousands of books, training videos, and prepublication manuscripts in one fully searchable database from publishers like O'Reilly Media, Prentice Hall Professional, Addison-Wesley Professional, Microsoft Press, Sams, Que, Peachpit Press, Focal Press, Cisco Press, John Wiley & Sons, Syngress, Morgan Kaufmann, IBM Redbooks, Packt, Adobe Press, FT Press, Apress, Manning, New Riders, McGraw-Hill, Jones & Bartlett, Course Technology, and dozens more. For more information about Safari Books Online, please visit us online.

How to Contact Us

Please address comments and questions concerning this book to the publisher:

O'Reilly Media, Inc.
1005 Gravenstein Highway North
Sebastopol, CA 95472
800-998-9938 (in the United States or Canada)
707-829-0515 (international or local)
707-829-0104 (fax)

We have a web page for this book, where we list errata, examples, and any additional information. You can access this page at *http://oreil.ly/Prog-Elastic-MapReduce*.

To comment or ask technical questions about this book, send email to *bookques tions@oreilly.com*.

For more information about our books, courses, conferences, and news, see our website at *http://www.oreilly.com*.

Find us on Facebook: *http://facebook.com/oreilly*

Follow us on Twitter: *http://twitter.com/oreillymedia*

Watch us on YouTube: *http://www.youtube.com/oreillymedia*

Acknowledgments

My wife Michelle gave me the encouragement to complete this book. Of course my employer, Dell, deserves an acknowledgment. They provided me with support to do this project. I next need to thank my co-workers who provided me with valuable input: Rob Scudiere, Wayne Haber, and Marco Arguedas. Finally, the tech reviewers provided fantastic guidance on how to make the book better: Jennifer Davis, Michael Ducy, Kirk Kimmel, Ari Hershowitz, Chris Corriere, Matthew Gast, and Russell Jurney.

—Kevin

I would like to thank my beautiful wife, Inna, and my lovely children Jacqueline and Josephine. Their kindness, humor, and love gave me inspiration and support while writing this book and through all of life's adventures. I would also like to thank the tech reviewers for their insightful feedback that greatly improved many of the learning examples in the book. Matthew Gast, in particular, provided great feedback throughout all sections of the book, and his insights into the business and technical merits of the technologies and examples were invaluable. Wayne Haber, Rob Scudiere, Jim Birmingham, and my employer Dell deserve acknowledgment for their valuable input and regular reviews throughout the development of the book. I would finally like to thank my co-author Kevin Schmidt and my editor Courtney Nash for giving the opportunity to be part of this great book and their hard work and efforts in its development.

—Chris

CHAPTER 1

Introduction to Amazon Elastic MapReduce

In programming, as in many fields, the hard part isn't solving problems, but deciding what problems to solve.

— Paul Graham
Great Hackers

On August 6, 2012, the Mars rover *Curiosity* landed on the red planet millions of miles from Earth. A great deal of engineering and technical expertise went into this mission. Just as exciting was the information technology behind this mission and the use of AWS services by the NASA's Jet Propulsion Laboratory (JPL) (*http://aws.amazon.com/solu tions/case-studies/nasa-jpl-curiosity/*). Shortly before the landing, NASA was able to provision stacks of AWS (*http://aws.amazon.com/solutions/case-studies/nasa-jpl-curiosity/*) infrastructure to support 25 Gbps of throughput to provide NASA's many fans and scientists up-to-the-minute information about the rover and its landing. Today, NASA continues to use AWS to analyze data and give scientists quick access to scientific data from the mission.

Why is this an important event in a book about Amazon Elastic MapReduce? Access to these types of resources used to be available only to governments or very large multinational corporations. Now this power to analyze volumes of data and support high volumes of traffic in an instant is available to anyone with a laptop and a credit card. What used to take months—with the buildout of large data centers, computing hardware, and networking—can now be done in an instant and for short-term projects in AWS.

Today, businesses need to understand their customers and identify trends to stay ahead of their competition. In finance and corporate security, businesses are being inundated with terabytes and petabytes of information. IT departments with tight budgets are being asked to make sense of the ever-growing amount of data and help businesses stay ahead of the game. Hadoop and the MapReduce framework have been powerful tools to help in this fight. However, this has not eliminated the cost and time needed to build out and maintain vast IT infrastructure to do this work in the traditional data center.

EMR is an in-the-cloud solution hosted in Amazon's data center that supplies both the computing horsepower and the on-demand infrastructure needed to solve these complex issues of finding trends and understanding vast volumes of data.

Throughout this book, we will explore Amazon EMR and how you can use it to solve data analysis problems in your organization. In many of the examples, we will focus on a common problem many organizations face: analyzing computer log information across multiple disparate systems. Many businesses are required by compliance regulations that exist, such as the Health Insurance Portability and Accountability Act (HIPAA) and the Payment Card Industry Data Security Standard (PCI DSS), to analyze and review log information on a regular, if not daily, basis. Log information from a large enterprise can easily grow into terabytes or petabytes of data. We will build a number of building blocks of an application that takes in computer log information and analyzes it for trends utilizing EMR. We will show you how to utilize Amazon EMR services to perform this analysis and discuss the economics and costs of doing so.

Amazon Web Services Used in This Book

AWS has grown greatly over the years from its origins as a provider of remotely hosted infrastructure with virtualized computer instances called Amazon Elastic Compute Cloud (EC2). Today, AWS provides many, if not all, of the building blocks used in many applications today. Throughout this book, we will focus on a number of the key services Amazon provides.

Amazon Elastic MapReduce (EMR)
> A book focused on EMR would not be complete without using this key AWS service from Amazon. We will go into much greater detail throughout this book, but in short, Amazon EMR is the in-the-cloud workhorse of the Hadoop framework that allows us to analyze vast amounts of data with a configurable and scalable amount of computing power. Amazon EMR makes heavy use of the Amazon Simple Storage Service (S3) to store analysis results and host data sets for processing, and leverages Amazon EC2's scalable compute resources to run the Job Flows we develop to perform analysis. There is an additional charge of about 30 percent for the EMR EC2 instances. To read Amazon's overview of EMR, visit the Amazon EMR web page (*http://aws.amazon.com/elasticmapreduce/*). As the primary focus of this book, Amazon EMR is used heavily in many of the examples.

Amazon Simple Storage Service (S3)
> Amazon S3 is the persistent storage for AWS. It provides a simple web services interface that can be used to store and retrieve any amount of data, at any time, from anywhere on the Web. There are some restrictions, though; data in S3 must

be stored in named buckets, and any single object can be no more than 5 terabytes in size. The data stored in S3 is highly durable and is stored in multiple facilities and multiple devices within a facility. Throughout this book, we will use S3 storage to store many of the Amazon EMR scripts, source data, and the results of our analysis.

As with almost all AWS services, there are standard REST- and SOAP-based web service APIs to interact with files stored on S3. It gives any developer access to the same highly scalable, reliable, secure, fast, inexpensive infrastructure that Amazon uses to run its own global network of websites. The service aims to maximize benefits of scale and to pass those benefits on to developers. To read Amazon's overview of S3, visit the Amazon S3 web page (*http://aws.amazon.com/s3/*). Amazon S3's permanent storage will be used to store data sets and computed result sets generated by Amazon EMR Job Flows. Applications built with Amazon EMR will need to use some S3 services for data storage.

Amazon Elastic Compute Cloud (EC2)

Amazon EC2 makes it possible to run multiple instances of virtual machines on demand inside any one of the AWS regions. The beauty of this service is that you can start as many or as few instances as you need without having to buy or rent physical hardware like in traditional hosting services. In the case of Amazon EMR, this means we can scale the size of our Hadoop cluster to any size we need without thinking about new hardware purchases and capacity planning. Individual EC2 instances come in a variety of sizes and specifications to meet the needs of different types of applications. There are instances tailored for high CPU load, high memory, high I/O, and more. Throughout this book, we will use native EC2 instances for a lot of the scheduling of Amazon EMR Job Flows and to run many of the mundane administrative and data manipulation tasks associated with our application building blocks. We will, of course, be using the Amazon EMR EC2 instances to do the heavy data crunching and analysis.

To read Amazon's overview of EC2, visit the Amazon EC2 web page (*http://aws.amazon.com/ec2/*). Amazon EC2 instances are used as part of an Amazon EMR cluster throughout the book. We also utilize EC2 instances for administrative functions and to simulate live traffic and data sets. In building your own application, you can run the administrative and live data on your own internal hosts, and these separate EC2 instances are not a required service in building an application with Amazon EMR.

Amazon Glacier

Amazon Glacier is a new offering available in AWS. Glacier is similar to S3 in that it stores almost any amount of data in a secure and durable manner. Glacier is intended for long-term storage of data due to the high latency involved in the storage and retrieval of data. A request to retrieve data from Glacier may take several hours for Amazon to fulfill. For this reason, we will store data that we do not intend to use very often in Amazon Glacier. The benefit of Amazon Glacier is its large cost savings. At the time of this writing, the storage cost in the US East region was $0.01 per gigabyte per month. Comparing this to a cost of $0.076 to $0.095 per gigabyte per month for S3 storage, you can see how the cost savings will add up for large amounts of data. To read Amazon's overview of Glacier, visit the Amazon Glacier web page (*http://aws.amazon.com/glacier/*). Glacier can be used to reduce data storage costs over S3, but is not a required service in building an Amazon EMR application.

Amazon Data Pipeline

Amazon Data Pipeline is another new offering available in AWS. Data Pipeline is a web service that allows us to build graphical workflows to reliably process and move data between different AWS services. Data Pipeline allows us to create complex user-defined logic to control AWS resource usage and execution of tasks. It allows the user to define schedules, prerequisite conditions, and dependencies to build an operational workflow for AWS. To read Amazon's overview of Data Pipeline, visit the Amazon Data Pipeline web page (*http://aws.amazon.com/datapipe line/*). Data Pipeline can reduce the overall administrative costs of an application using Amazon EMR, but is not a required AWS service for building an application.

Amazon Elastic MapReduce

Amazon EMR is an AWS service that allows users to launch and use resizable Hadoop clusters inside of Amazon's infrastructure. Amazon EMR, like Hadoop, can be used to analyze large data sets. It greatly simplifies the setup and management of the cluster of Hadoop and MapReduce components. EMR instances use Amazon's prebuilt and customized EC2 instances, which can take full advantage of Amazon's infrastructure and other AWS services. These EC2 instances are invoked when we start a new Job Flow to form an EMR cluster. A *Job Flow* is Amazon's term for the complete data processing that occurs through a number of compute steps in Amazon EMR. A Job Flow is specified by the MapReduce application and its input and output parameters.

Figure 1-1 shows an architectural view of the EMR cluster.

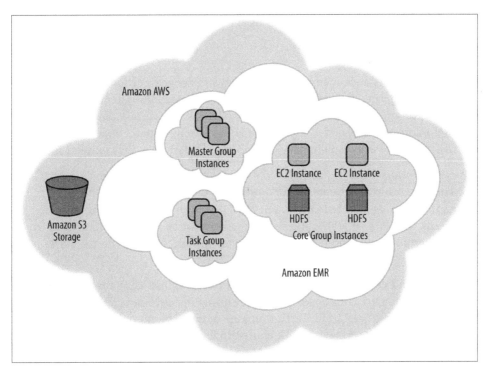

Figure 1-1. Typical Amazon EMR cluster

Amazon EMR performs the computational analysis using the MapReduce (*http://wiki.apache.org/hadoop/MapReduce*) framework. The MapReduce framework splits the input data into smaller fragments, or shards, that are distributed to the nodes that compose the cluster. From Figure 1-1, we note that a Job Flow is executed on a series of EC2 instances running the Hadoop components that are broken up into master, core, and task clusters. These individual data fragments are then processed by the MapReduce application running on each of the core and task nodes in the cluster. Based on Amazon EMR terminology, we commonly call the MapReduce application a Job Flow throughout this book.

The master, core, and task cluster groups perform the following key functions in the Amazon EMR cluster:

Master group instance
> The master group instance manages the Job Flow and allocates all the needed executables, JARs, scripts, and data shards to the core and task instances. The master node monitors the health and status of the core and task instances and also collects the data from these instances and writes it back to Amazon S3. The master group instances serve a critical function in our Amazon EMR cluster. If a master node is

lost, you lose the work in progress by the master *and* the core and task nodes to which it had delegated work.

Core group instance

Core group instance members run the map and reduce portions of our Job Flow, and store intermediate data to the Hadoop Distributed File System (HDFS) storage in our Amazon EMR cluster. The master node manages the tasks and data delegated to the core and task nodes. Due to the HDFS storage aspects of core nodes, a loss of a core node will result in data loss and possible failure of the complete Job Flow.

Task group instance

The task group is optional. It can do some of the dirty computational work of the map and reduce jobs, but does not have HDFS storage of the data and intermediate results. The lack of HDFS storage on these instances means the data needs to be transferred to these nodes by the master for the task group to do the work in the Job Flow.

The master and core group instances are critical components in the Amazon EMR cluster. A loss of a node in the master or core group instance can cause an application to fail and need to be restarted. Task groups are optional because they do not control a critical function of the Amazon EMR cluster. In terms of jobs and responsibilities, the master group must maintain the status of tasks. A loss of a node in the master group may make it so the status of a running task cannot be determined or retrieved and lead to Job Flow failure.

The core group runs tasks and maintains the data retained in the Amazon EMR cluster. A loss of a core group node may cause data loss and Job Flow failure.

A task node is only responsible for running tasks delegated to it from the master group and utilizes data maintained by the core group. A failure of a task node will lose any interim calculations. The master node will retry the task node when it detects failure in the running job. Because task group nodes do not control the state of jobs or maintain data in the Amazon EMR cluster, task nodes are optional, but they are one of the key areas where capacity of the Amazon EMR cluster can be expanded or shrunk without affecting the stability of the cluster.

Amazon EMR and the Hadoop Ecosystem

As we've already seen, Amazon EMR uses Hadoop and its MapReduce framework at its core. Accordingly, many of the other core Apache Software Foundation projects that work with Hadoop also work with Amazon EMR. There are also many other AWS services that may be useful when you're running and monitoring Amazon EMR applications. Some of these will be covered briefly in this book:

Hive

Hive is a distributed data warehouse that allows you to create a Job Flow using a SQL-like language. Hive can be run from a script loaded in S3 or interactively inside of a running EMR instance. We will explore Hive in Chapter 4.

Pig

Pig is a data flow language. (The language is, not surprisingly, called Pig Latin.) Pig scripts can be loaded into S3 and used to perform the data analysis in a Job Flow. Pig, like Hive, is one of the Job Flow types that can be run interactively inside of a running EMR instance. We cover the details on Pig and Pig Latin in Chapter 3.

Amazon Cloudwatch

Cloudwatch allows you to monitor the health and progress of Job Flows. It also allows you to set alarms when metrics are outside of normal execution parameters. We will look at Amazon Cloudwatch briefly in Chapter 6.

Amazon Elastic MapReduce Versus Traditional Hadoop Installs

So how does using Amazon EMR compare to building out Hadoop in the traditional data center? Many of the AWS cloud considerations we discuss in Appendix B are also relevant to Amazon EMR. Compared to allocating resources and buying hardware in a traditional data center, Amazon EMR can be a great place to start a project because the infrastructure is already available at Amazon. Let's look at a number of key areas that you should consider before embarking on a new Amazon EMR project.

Data Locality

Amazon EMR uses S3 storage for the input and output of data sets to be processed and analyzed. In order to process data, you need to transport it from the many sources where it currently lives up to Amazon's cloud into S3 buckets. This is not a major issue for projects transitioning from other AWS services, but may be a barrier to projects that need to transport terabytes or petabytes of data from another cloud provider or hosted in a private data center to Amazon's S3 storage.

In the traditional Hadoop install, data transport between the current source locations and the Hadoop cluster may be colocated in the same data center on high-speed internal networks. This lowers the data transport barriers and the amount of time to get data into Hadoop for analysis. Figure 1-2 shows the data locations and network topology differences between an Amazon EMR and traditional Hadoop installation.

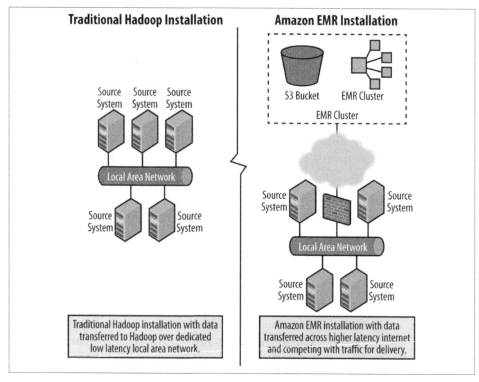

Traditional Hadoop Installation

Source System Source System Source System

Local Area Network

Source System Source System

Traditional Hadoop installation with data transferred to Hadoop over dedicated low latency local area network.

Amazon EMR Installation

S3 Bucket EMR Cluster

EMR Cluster

Source System Source System

Local Area Network

Source System Source System

Amazon EMR installation with data transferred across higher latency internet and competing with traffic for delivery.

Figure 1-2. Comparing data locality between Hadoop and Amazon EMR environments

If this will be a large factor in your project, you should review Amazon's S3 Import and Export (*http://aws.amazon.com/importexport/*) service option. The Import and Export service for S3 allows you to prepare portable storage devices that you can ship to Amazon to import your data into S3. This can greatly decrease the time and costs associated with getting large data sets into S3 for analysis. This approach can also be used in transitioning a project to AWS and EMR to seed the existing data into S3 and add data updates as they occur.

Hardware

Many people point to Hadoop's use of low-cost hardware to achieve enormous compute capacity as one of the great benefits of using Hadoop compared to purchasing large, specialized hardware configurations. We couldn't agree more when comparing what Hadoop achieves in terms of cost and compute capacity in this model. However, there are still large upfront costs in building out a modest Hadoop cluster. There are also the ongoing operational costs of electricity, cooling, IT personnel, hardware retirement, capacity planning and buildout, and vendor maintenance contracts on the operating system and hardware.

With Amazon EMR, you only pay for the services you use. You can quickly scale capacity up and down, and if you need more memory or CPU for your application, this is a simple change in your EC2 instance types when you're creating a new Job Flow. We'll explore the costs of Amazon EMR in Chapter 6 and help you understand how to estimate costs to determine the best solution for your organization.

Complexity

With the low-cost hardware of Hadoop clusters, many organizations start proof-of-concept data analysis projects with a small Hadoop cluster. The success of these projects leads many organizations to start building out their clusters and meet production-level data needs. These projects eventually reach a tipping point of complexity where much of the cost savings gained from the low-cost hardware is lost to the administrative, labor, and data center cost burdens. The time and labor commitments of keeping thousands of Hadoop nodes updated with OS security patches and replacing failing systems can require a great deal of time and IT resources. Estimating them and being able to compare these costs to EMR will be covered in detail in Chapter 6.

With Amazon EMR, the EMR cluster nodes exist and are maintained by Amazon. Amazon regularly updates its EC2 Amazon Machine Images (AMI) with newer releases of Hadoop, security patches, and more. By default, a Job Flow will start an EMR cluster with the latest and greatest EC2 AMIs. This removes much of the administrative burden in running and maintaining large Hadoop clusters for data analysis.

Application Building Blocks

In order to show the power of using AWS for building applications, we will build a number of building blocks for a MapReduce log analysis application. In many of our examples throughout this book, we will use these building blocks to perform analysis of common computer logfiles and demonstrate how these same building blocks can be used to attack other common data analysis problems. We will discuss how AWS and Amazon EMR can be utilized to solve different aspects of these analysis problems. Figure 1-3 shows the high-level functional diagram of the AWS components we will use in the upcoming chapters. Figure 1-3 also highlights the workflow and inter-relationships between these components and how they share data and communicate in the AWS infrastructure.

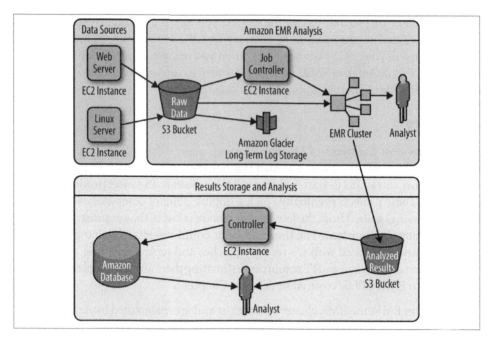

Figure 1-3. Functional architecture of our data analysis solution

Using our building blocks, we will explore how these can be used to ingest large volumes of log data, perform real-time and batch analysis, and ultimately produce results that can be shared with end users. We will derive meaning and understanding from data and produce actionable results. There are three component areas for the application: collection stage, analysis stage, and the nuts and bolts of how we coordinate and schedule work through the many services we use. It might seem like a complex set of systems, interconnections, storage, and so on, but it's really quite simple, and Amazon EMR and AWS provide us a number of great tools, services, and utilities to solve complex data analysis problems.

In the next set of chapters, we will dive into each component area of the application and highlight key portions of solving data analysis problems:

Collection

In Chapter 2, we will work on data collection attributes that are the key building blocks for any data analysis project. We will present a number of small AWS options for generating test data to work with and learn about working with this data in Amazon EMR and S3. Chapter 2 will explore real-world areas to collect data throughout your enterprise and the tools available to get this data into Amazon S3.

Analysis

In Chapters 2 and 3, we will begin analyzing the data we have collected using Java code to write map and reduce methods that will be run as Job Flows in Amazon

EMR. In Chapter 4, we will show you that you don't have to be a NASA rocket scientist or a Java programmer to use Amazon EMR. We will revisit the same analysis issues covered in earlier chapters, and using more high-level scripting tools like Pig and Hive, solve the same problems. Hadoop and Amazon EMR allow us to bring to bear a significant number of tools to mine critical information out of our data.

Machine learning

In Chapter 5, we will explore how machine learning can be used in EMR to derive interesting results on data sets. Python is used for the examples in this chapter.

Storage

Storage and the costs of storing data are always an ever-growing problem for organizations. After you have done your data analysis, you may need to retain the original data and analysis for many years. Depending on the compliance needs of an organization, the retention time can be very long. In Chapter 6, we will look at cost-effective ways to store data for long periods using Amazon Glacier (*http:// aws.amazon.com/glacier/*).

By now, you hopefully have an understanding of how AWS and Amazon EMR could provide value to your organization. In the next chapter, you will start getting your hands dirty. You'll generate some simple log data to analyze and create your first Amazon EMR Job Flow, and then do some simple data frequency analysis on those sample log messages.

CHAPTER 2

Data Collection and Data Analysis with AWS

Now that we've covered the basics of AWS and Amazon EMR, you can get to work on using Amazon's tools in the cloud. To get started, you'll create some sample data to parse your first Amazon EMR job. A number of AWS tools and techniques will be required as part of this exercise to move the data to a location that Amazon EMR can access and work on. This should give you a solid background on what is available, and how to begin thinking about your data and overcoming challenges of moving your data into AWS.

Amazon EMR is built with many' of the core components and frameworks of Apache Hadoop (*http://hadoop.apache.org/*). Apache Hadoop allows organizations to build data-intensive distributed applications across a cluster of low-cost hardware. Amazon EMR simply takes this technology and moves it to the Amazon cloud to run at web scale on Amazon's AWS hardware.

The key to all of this is the MapReduce framework. MapReduce is a powerful framework used to break down large data sets into smaller sets that can be processed in Amazon EMR across multiple EC2 instances that compose a cluster. To demonstrate the power of this concept, in this chapter you'll create an Amazon EMR Cluster, also known as a Job Flow in Java. The Job Flow will determine message frequency for the test sample data set. Of course, as with learning anything new, you are bound to make mistakes and errors in the development of an Amazon EMR Job Flow. Toward the end of the chapter, we will intentionally introduce a number of errors into the Job Flow so you can step through the process of exploring Amazon EMR logs and tools. This process can help you find errors and resolve problems in your own Amazon EMR application.

Log Analysis Application

Now let's focus on building a number of the components of the log analysis application described in Chapter 1. You will create your data set in the cloud on a Linux system using Amazon's EC2 service. Then the data will be moved through S3 to be processed by an application running on the Amazon EMR cluster, and in the end the processed result set will show the error messages and their frequency. Figure 2-1 shows the workflow of the system components that you'll be building.

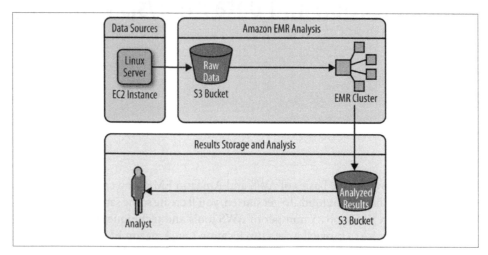

Figure 2-1. Application workflow covered in this chapter

Log Messages as a Data Set for Analytics

Since the growth of the Internet, the amount of electronic data that companies retain has exploded. With the advent of tools like Amazon EMR, it is only recently that companies have had tools to mine and use their vast data repositories. Companies are using their data sets to gain a competitive advantage over their rivals by mining their data sets to learn what matters to their customer base the most. The growth in this field has put data scientists and individuals with data analytics skills in high demand.

The struggle many have faced is how to get started learning with these tools and access a data set of sufficient size. This is why we have chosen to use computer log messages to illustrate many of the points in the first Job Flow example in this chapter. Computers are logging information on a regular basis, and the logfiles are a ready and available data source that most developers understand well from troubleshooting issues in their daily jobs. Computer logfiles are a great data source to start learning how to use data analysis tools like Amazon EMR. Take a look at your own computer—on a Linux or Macintosh system, many of the logfiles can be found in */var/log*. Figure 2-2 shows an example of the format and information of some of the log messages that you can find.

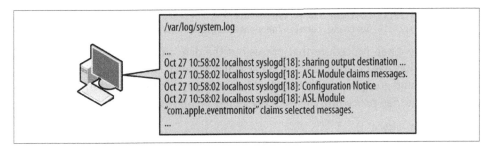

```
/var/log/system.log

...
Oct 27 10:58:02 localhost syslogd[18]: sharing output destination ...
Oct 27 10:58:02 localhost syslogd[18]: ASL Module claims messages.
Oct 27 10:58:02 localhost syslogd[18]: Configuration Notice
Oct 27 10:58:02 localhost syslogd[18]: ASL Module
"com.apple.eventmonitor" claims selected messages.
...
```

Figure 2-2. Typical computer log messages

If this data set does not work well for you and your industry, Amazon hosts many public data sets (*http://aws.amazon.com/datasets*) that you could use instead. The data science website Kaggle (*http://www.kaggle.com/*) also hosts a number of data science competitions that may be another useful resource for data sets as you are learning about MapReduce.

Understanding MapReduce

Before getting too far into an example, let's explore the basics of MapReduce. MapReduce is the core of Hadoop, and hence the same is true for Amazon EMR. MapReduce is the programming model that allows Amazon EMR to take massive amounts of data, break it up into small chunks across a configured number of virtual EC2 instances, analyze the data in parallel across the instances using map and reduce procedures that we write, and derive conclusions from analyses on very large data sets.

The term *MapReduce* refers to the separate procedures written to build a MapReduce application that perform analysis on the data. The map procedure takes a chunk of data as input and filters and sorts the data down to a set of key/value pairs that will be processed by the reduce procedure. The reduce procedure performs summary procedures of grouping, sorting, or counting of the key/value pairs, and allows Amazon EMR to process and analyze very large data sets across multiple EC2 instances that compose an Amazon EMR cluster.

Let's take a look at how MapReduce works using a sample log entry as an example. Let's say you would like to know how many log messages are created every second. This can be useful in numerous data analysis problems, from determining load distribution, pinpointing network hotspots, or gathering performance data, to finding machines that may be under attack. In general, these sorts of issues fall into a category commonly referred to as *frequency analysis*. Looking at the example log record, the time in the log messages is the first data element and notes when the message occurred down to the second:

```
Apr 15 23:27:14 hostname.local ./generate-log.sh[17580]: INFO: Login ...
Apr 15 23:27:14 hostname.local ./generate-log.sh[17580]: INFO: Login ...
```

```
Apr 15 23:27:15 hostname.local ./generate-log.sh[17580]: WARNING: Login failed...
Apr 15 23:27:16 hostname.local ./generate-log.sh[17580]: INFO: Login ...
```

We can write a map procedure that parses out the date and time and treats this data element as a key. We can then use the key selected, which is the date and time in the log data, to sort and group the log entries that have occurred at that timestamp. The pseudocode for the map procedure can be represented as follows:

```
map( "Log Record" )
    Parse Date and Time
    Emit Date and Time as the key with a value of 1
```

The map procedure would emit a set of key/value pairs like the following items:

```
(Apr 15 23:27:14, 1)
(Apr 15 23:27:14, 1)
(Apr 15 23:27:15, 1)
(Apr 15 23:27:16, 1)
...
```

This simple map procedure parses a log line, emits the date and time as the key, and uses the numeric value of one as the value in each pair. The data set generated by the map procedure is grouped by the framework to combine duplicate keys and create an array of values for each key. The following is the final intermediate data set that is sent to the reduce procedure:

```
(Apr 15 23:27:14, (1, 1))
(Apr 15 23:27:15, 1)
(Apr 15 23:27:16, 1)
...
```

The reduce procedure determines a count of each key—date and time—by iterating through the array of values and coming up with the total number of the log lines that occurred each second. The pseudocode for the reduce procedure can be represented something like the following:

```
reduce( Key, Values )
  sum = 0
  for each Value:
    sum = sum + value
  emit (Key, sum)
```

The reduce procedure will generate a single line with the key and sum for each key as follows:

```
Apr 15 23:27:14 2
Apr 15 23:27:15 1
Apr 15 23:27:16 1
...
```

The final result from the reduce procedure has gone through each of the date and time keys from the map procedure and arrived at counts for the number of log lines that occurred on each second in the sample logfile.

Figure 2-3 details the flow of data through the map and reduce phases of a Job Flow working on the log data.

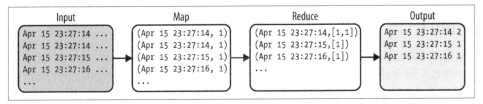

Figure 2-3. Data Flow through the map and reduce framework components

Collection Stage

To utilize the power of Amazon EMR, we need a data set to perform analysis on. AWS services as well as Amazon EMR utilize Amazon S3 for persistent storage and data retrieval. Let's get a data set loaded into S3 so you can start your analysis.

The collection stage is the first step in any data analysis problem. Your first challenge as a data scientist is to get access to raw data from the systems that contain it and pull it into a location where it can actually be analyzed. In many organizations, data will come in flat files, databases, and binary formats stored in many locations. Recalling the log analysis example described in Chapter 1, we know there is a wide diversity of log sources and log formats in an enterprise organization:

- Servers (Unix, Windows, etc.)
- Firewalls
- Intrusion detection systems (IDS)
- Printers
- Proxy servers
- Web application firewalls (WAF)
- Custom-built software

In the traditional setting, the data will be fed into the data analysis system with raw data from applications, devices, and systems on an internal corporate network. In today's environments, it is conceivable that the data to be processed will be distributed on internal networks, extranets, and even applications and sources running in a cloud environment already. These systems are all good and realistic sources of data for data analysis problems in an organization.

In this section, you'll provision and start an EC2 instance to generate some sample raw log data. In order to keep the data collection simple, we'll generate a syslog format log file on the EC2 instance. These same utilities can be used to load data from the various source systems in a typical organization into an S3 bucket for analysis.

Simulating Syslog Data

The simplest way to get started is to generate a set of log data from the command line utilizing a Bash shell script. The data will have relatively regular frequency because the Bash script is just generating log data in a loop and the data itself is not user- or event-driven. We'll look at a data set generated from system- and user-driven data in Chapter 3 after the basic Amazon EMR analysis concepts are covered here.

Let's create and start an Amazon Linux EC2 instance on which to run a Bash script. From the Amazon AWS Management Console (*https://console.aws.amazon.com/console/home*), choose the EC2 service to start the process of creating a running Linux instance in AWS. Figure 2-4 shows the EC2 Services Management Console.

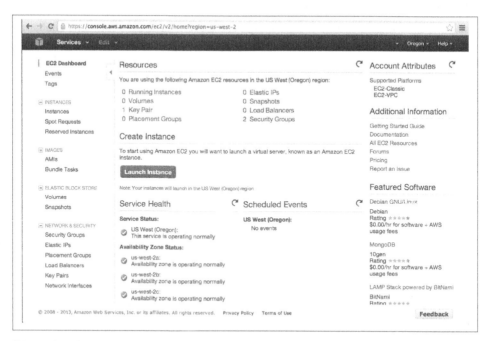

Figure 2-4. Amazon EC2 Services Management Console

From this page, choose Launch Instance to start the process of creating a new EC2 instance. You have a large number of types of EC2 instances to choose from, and many of them will sound similar to systems and setups running in a traditional data center. These choices are broken up based on the operating system installed, the platform type of 32-bit or 64-bit, and the amount of memory and CPU that will be allocated to the new EC2 instance. The various memory and CPU allocation options sound a lot like fast food restaurant meal size choices of micro, small, medium, large, extra large, double extra large, and so on. To learn more about EC2 instance types and what size may make sense for your application, see more at Amazon's EC2 website (*http://aws.amazon.com/ ec2/instance-types/*), where Amazon describes the sizing options and pricing available.

Speed and resource constraints are not important considerations for generating the simple syslog data set from a Bash script. We will be creating a new EC2 instance that uses the Amazon Linux AMI. This image type is shown in the EC2 creation wizard in Figure 2-5. After choosing the operating system we will create the smallest option, the micro instance. This EC2 machine size is sufficient to get started generating log data.

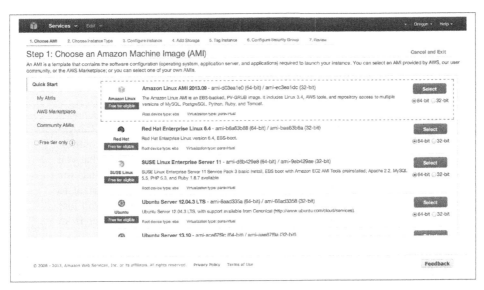

Figure 2-5. Amazon Linux AMI EC2 instance creation

After you've gone through Amazon's instance creation wizard, the new EC2 instance is created and running in the AWS cloud. The running instance will appear in the Amazon EC2 Management Console as shown in Figure 2-6. You can now establish a connection to the running Linux instance through a variety of tools based on the operating system chosen. On running Linux instances, you can establish a connection directly through a web browser by choosing the Connect option available on the right-click menu after you've selected the running EC2 instance.

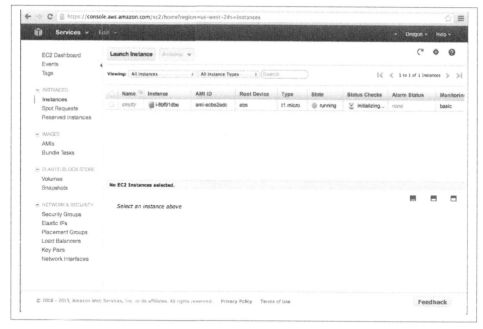

Figure 2-6. The created Amazon EC2 micro instance in the EC2 Console

 Amazon uses key pairs as a way of accessing EC2 instances and a number of other AWS services. The key pair (*http://bit.ly/EC2-KP-AMECC*) is part of the SSL encryption mechanism used for communication between you and your cloud resources. It is critical that you keep the private key in a secure place because anyone who has the private key can access your cloud resources. It is also important to know that Amazon keeps a copy of your public key only. If you lose your private key, you have no way of retrieving it again later from Amazon.

Generating Logs with Bash

Now that an EC2 Linux image is up and running in AWS, let's create some log messages. The following simple Bash script will generate output similar to syslog-formatted messages found on a variety of other systems throughout an organization:

```
#!/bin/bash

log_message()
{
        Current_Date=`date +'%b %d %H:%M:%S'`
        Host=`hostname`
```

```
        echo "$Current_Date $Host $0[$$]: $1" >> $2  ❶
}

# Generate a log events
for (( i = 1; i <= $1 ; i++ ))  ❷
do
    log_message "INFO: Login successful for user Alice" $2  ❸
    log_message "INFO: Login successful for user Bob" $2
    log_message "WARNING: Login failed for user Mallory" $2
    log_message "SEVERE: Received SEGFAULT signal from process Eve" $2
    log_message "INFO: Logout occurred for user Alice" $2
    log_message "INFO: User Walter accessed file /var/log/messages" $2
    log_message "INFO: Login successful for user Chuck" $2
    log_message "INFO: Password updated for user Craig" $2
    log_message "SEVERE: Disk write failure" $2
    log_message "SEVERE: Unable to complete transaction - Out of memory" $2  ❹
done
```

❶ Generates a syslog-like log message

❷ The first parameter ($1) passed to the Bash script; we can specify any number of log line iterations

❸ The second parameter ($2) specifies the log output filename

❹ The output we selected was a pseudo-output stream of items you may find in a logfile

With the Bash script loaded into the new EC2 instance, you can run the script to generate some test log data for Amazon EMR to work with later in this chapter. In this example, the Bash script was stored as *generate-log.sh*. The example run of the script will generate 1,000 iterations or 10,000 lines of log output to a logfile named *sample-syslog.log*:

```
$ chmod +x generate-log.sh
$ generate-log.sh 1000 ./sample-syslog.log
```

Let's examine the output the script generated. Opening the logfile created by the Bash script, you can see a number of repetitive log lines are created, as shown in Example 2-1. There will be some variety in the frequency of these messages based on other processes running on the EC2 instance and other EC2 instances running on the same physical hardware as our EC2 instance. You can find a little more detail on how other cloud users affect the execution of applications in Appendix B.

Example 2-1. Generated sample syslog

```
Apr 15 23:27:14 hostname.local ./generate-log.sh[17580]: INFO: Login
successful for user Alice
Apr 15 23:27:14 hostname.local ./generate-log.sh[17580]: INFO: Login
successful for user Bob
Apr 15 23:27:14 hostname.local ./generate-log.sh[17580]: WARNING: Login
failed for user Mallory
```

```
Apr 15 23:27:14 hostname.local ./generate-log.sh[17580]: SEVERE: Received
SEGFAULT signal from process Eve
Apr 15 23:27:14 hostname.local ./generate-log.sh[17580]: INFO: Logout
occurred for user Alice
Apr 15 23:27:14 hostname.local ./generate-log.sh[17580]: INFO: User
Walter accessed file /var/log/messages
Apr 15 23:27:14 hostname.local ./generate-log.sh[17580]: INFO: Login
successful for user Chuck
Apr 15 23:27:14 hostname.local ./generate-log.sh[17580]: INFO: Password
updated for user Craig
Apr 15 23:27:14 hostname.local ./generate-log.sh[17580]: SEVERE: Disk write failure
Apr 15 23:27:14 hostname.local ./generate-log.sh[17580]: SEVERE:
to complete transaction - Out of memory
```

Diving briefly into the details of the components that compose a single log line will help you understand the format of a syslog message and how this data will be parsed by the Amazon EMR Job Flow. Looking at this log output also helps you understand how to think about the components of a message and the data elements needed in the MapReduce code that will be written to compute message frequency.

Apr 15 23:27:14
: This is the date and time the message was created. This is the item that will be used as a key for developing the counts that represent message frequency in the log.

hostname.local
: In a typical syslog message, this part of the message represents the hostname on which the message was generated.

generate-log.sh
: This represents the name of the process that generated the message in the logfile. The script in this example was stored as *generate-log.sh* in the running EC2 instance, and this is the name of the process in the logfile.

[17580]
: Typically, every running process is given a process ID that exists for the life of the running process. This number will vary based on the number of processes running on a machine.

SEVERE: Unable to complete transaction - Out of memory
: This represents the free-form description of the log message that is generated. In syslog messages, the messages and their meaning are typically dependent on the process generating the message. Some understanding of the process that generated the message is necessary to determine the criticality and meaning of the log message. This is a common problem in examining computer log information. Similar issues will exist in many data analysis problems when you're trying to derive meaning and correlation across multiple, disparate systems.

From the log analysis example application used to demonstrate AWS functionality throughout this book, we know there is tremendous diversity in log messages and their meaning. Syslog is the closest thing to a standard in logging when it comes to computer logs. Many would argue that it's a bit of a stretch to call syslog a standard, because there is still tremendous diversity in the log messages from system to system and vendor to vendor. However, a number of RFCs define the aspects and meaning of syslog messages. You should review RFC-3164 (*http://datatracker.ietf.org/doc/rfc3164/*), RFC-5452 (*http://tools.ietf.org/html/rfc5424*), and RFC-5427 (*http://tools.ietf.org/html/rfc5427*) to learn more about the critical aspects of syslog if you're building a similar application. Logging and log management is a very large problem area for many organizations, and *Logging and Log Management: The Authoritative Guide to Understanding the Concepts Surrounding Logging and Log Management* (*http://store.elsevier.com/Logging-and-Log-Management/Anton-Chuvakin/isbn-9781597496353/*), by Anton Chuvakin, Kevin Schmidt, and Christopher Phillips (Syngress), covers many aspects of the topic in great detail.

Moving Data to S3 Storage

A sample data set now exists in the running EC2 instance in Amazon's cloud. However, this data set is not in a location where it can be used in Amazon EMR because it is sitting on the local disk of a running EC2 instance. To make use of this data set, you'll need to move the data to S3, where Amazon EMR can access it. Amazon EMR will only work on data that is in an Amazon S3 storage location or is directly loaded into the HDFS storage in the Amazon EMR cluster.

Data in S3 is stored in buckets. An S3 bucket is a container for the objects, files, and directories of information that you store in it. S3 bucket names need to be globally unique, so choose your bucket name wisely. The bucket naming convention is a unique URL naming constraint. An S3 bucket can be referenced by URL to interact with S3 with the AWS REST API.

You have a number of methods for loading data into S3. A simple method of moving the log data into S3 is to use the s3cmd utility (*http://s3tools.org/s3cmd*):

```
hostname $ s3cmd --configure
```

For more information on installation and configuration of s3cmd, refer to the s3cmd website (*http://s3tools.org/s3cmd*). Let's go ahead and move the sample log data into S3. Example 2-2 shows a sample usage of s3cmd to load the test data into an S3 bucket named *program-emr*.

Example 2-2. Load data into an S3 bucket

```
hostname $ s3cmd mb s3://program-emr ❶
Bucket 's3://program-emr/' created
hostname $ s3cmd put sample-syslog.log s3://program-emr ❷
sample-syslog.log -> s3://program-emr/sample-syslog.log [1 of 1]
```

```
 988000 of 988000   100% in    0s     7.44 MB/s  done
hostname $
```

❶ Make a new bucket using the mb option. The new bucket created in the example
    is called *program-emr*.

❷ An s3cmd put is used to move the logfile *sample-syslog.log* into the S3 bucket
    program-emr.

All Roads Lead to S3

We chose the s3cmd utility to load the sample data into S3 because it can be used from
AWS resources and also from many of the systems located in private corporate networks.
Best of all, it is a tool that can be downloaded and configured to run in minutes to
transfer data up to S3 via a command line. But fear not: using a third-party unsupported
tool is not the only way of getting data into S3. The following list presents a number of
alternative methods of moving data to S3:

S3 Management Console (https://console.aws.amazon.com/s3/home)
>   S3, like many of the AWS services, has a management console that allows manage-
>   ment of the buckets and files in an AWS account. The management console allows
>   you to create new buckets, add and remove directories, upload new files, delete files,
>   update file permissions, and download files. Figure 2-7 shows the file uploaded into
>   S3 in the earlier examples inside the management console.

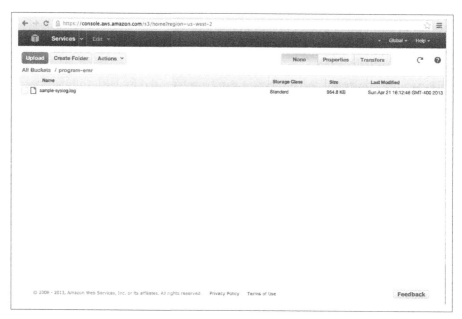

Figure 2-7. S3 Management Console

AWS SDK
> AWS comes with an extensive SDK for Java, .NET, Ruby, and numerous other programming languages. This allows interactions with S3 to load data and manipulation of S3 objects into third-party applications. Numerous S3 classes direct manipulation of objects and structures in S3. You may note that s3cmd source code (*https://github.com/s3tools/s3cmd*) is written in Python, and you can download the source from GitHub (*https://github.com/*).

S3 REST API (http://docs.aws.amazon.com/AmazonS3/latest/API/APIRest.html)
> S3 also has a REST API (*http://docs.aws.amazon.com/AmazonS3/latest/API/APIR est.html*) that allows for interaction with S3 using standard HTTP web service calls to manipulate S3 buckets and objects.

AWS Command Line Interface (http://aws.amazon.com/cli/)
> The AWS Command Line Interface (CLI) performs many of the same functions and features as s3cmd. Files can be uploaded and downloaded from S3 buckets. The utility also supports a sync feature to keep a local repository of objects stored in S3 in sync. This utility also supports controlling other AWS services like EC2. The full list of services supported by this utility are available on the AWS CLI reference page (*http://docs.aws.amazon.com/cli/latest/reference/*). At the time of writing this book, this utility had only recently come out of beta. The utility does not currently support controlling Amazon EMR services.

Developing a MapReduce Application

Amazon EMR and the underlying Hadoop frameworks it uses are built using the Java programming language. To turn the MapReduce pseudocode into a Custom JAR MapReduce Job Flow, you will need to have a system set up to do Java development and will need Hadoop Java JARs to build an application that Amazon EMR can consume and execute. To get ready to develop your first Amazon EMR, review Appendix C to set up your development environment.

Custom JAR MapReduce Job

Amazon EMR provides a number of ways to write map and reduce procedures, including Hive, Streaming, Pig, or Custom JAR. A number of these Job Flow types will be covered throughout this book. Because we are programmers at heart, let's start using Java to write a Custom JAR for the map and reduce procedures. Each of these EMR technology types can be used to analyze data as a computational step in the Amazon EMR Cluster. The set of steps run in Amazon EMR Cluster comprise a Job Flow for analyzing a dataset. Hive, Streaming, Pig, and Custom Jar are the Job Flow types that can be used as steps in an Amazon EMR cluster.

Now that the theory behind how the MapReduce framework has been covered, let's translate the pseudocode into a Custom JAR Job Flow written in Java. A JAR file is simply a compressed archive of compiled Java code. Writing Java applications for Amazon EMR follows the same pattern as writing applications for Hadoop. The code developed here will cover the map, reduce, and driver procedures. The driver procedure is the main entry point that wires together the Job Flow application and tells MapReduce the classes to use for map and reduce tasks. Translating the pseudocode into Java code creates a map function implementation as shown in Example 2-3.

Example 2-3. Mapper for counting log records per second

```java
import java.io.IOException;

import org.apache.hadoop.io.IntWritable;
import org.apache.hadoop.io.LongWritable;
import org.apache.hadoop.io.Text;
import org.apache.hadoop.mapred.MapReduceBase;
import org.apache.hadoop.mapred.Mapper;
import org.apache.hadoop.mapred.OutputCollector;
import org.apache.hadoop.mapred.Reporter;

public class LogMapper extends MapReduceBase
    implements Mapper<LongWritable, Text, Text, IntWritable>
{
    private Text word = new Text();
    private final static IntWritable one = new IntWritable( 1 );

    public void map( LongWritable key,
                    Text value,
                    OutputCollector<Text, IntWritable> output,
                    Reporter reporter) throws IOException
    {
        // Get the value as a String
        String text = value.toString();

        // Retrieve the date and time out of the log message, first 15 characters
        String SyslogDateTime = text.substring(0, 15);

        // Output the syslog date and time as the key and 1 as the value
        output.collect( new Text(SyslogDateTime), one );
    }
}
```

From this example, note that there are no special AWS classes or libraries used to write the map procedure. The Mapper interface comes from Hadoop Mapper imports in the simple LogMapper class.

The map method is passed a portion of the raw data file as input. The map method focuses on the value passed to it because this represents an individual row from the logfile. Looking at the sample data, we can see the date and time are the first 15 characters of each line of input. The map method will extract the date and time from the first 15 characters and use this as the key. The final portions of map procedure will emit the date and time key and a value of one for each line in the logfile.

Let's move on to the reduce procedure. The psuedocode can be translated into the reduce procedure in a similar fashion to Example 2-4.

Example 2-4. Reducer for counting log records per second

```
import java.io.IOException;
import java.util.Iterator;

import org.apache.hadoop.io.IntWritable;
import org.apache.hadoop.io.Text;
import org.apache.hadoop.mapred.MapReduceBase;
import org.apache.hadoop.mapred.OutputCollector;
import org.apache.hadoop.mapred.Reducer;
import org.apache.hadoop.mapred.Reporter;

public class LogReducer extends MapReduceBase
   implements Reducer<Text, IntWritable, Text, IntWritable>
{
    public void reduce( Text key, Iterator<IntWritable> values,
            OutputCollector<Text, IntWritable> output,
            Reporter reporter) throws IOException
    {
        // Counts the occurrences of the date and time
        int count = 0;
        while( values.hasNext() )
        {
                // Add the value to our count
                count += values.next().get();
        }

        // Output the date and time with its count
        output.collect( key, new IntWritable( count ) );
    }
}
```

The reduce method passes an iterator for the value parameter. This iterator points to the array of values for each key the method receives. The value of each element is not relevant for the reducer in this simple example because every value is set to the value of one. The reduce method simply iterates through and counts the number of elements in the array that are of the same key—namely, date and time.

The final piece wires all these procedures together and is the main entry point for the Job Flow. The driver method defines the map and reduce methods to use in the Amazon EMR Job Flow, as shown in Example 2-5.

Example 2-5. Driver class for the log analyzer MapReduce Job Flow

```java
import org.apache.hadoop.conf.Configured;
import org.apache.hadoop.fs.Path;
import org.apache.hadoop.io.IntWritable;
import org.apache.hadoop.io.Text;
import org.apache.hadoop.mapred.FileInputFormat;
import org.apache.hadoop.mapred.FileOutputFormat;
import org.apache.hadoop.mapred.JobClient;
import org.apache.hadoop.mapred.JobConf;
import org.apache.hadoop.util.Tool;
import org.apache.hadoop.util.ToolRunner;

public class LogAnalysisDriver extends Configured implements Tool {

        public int run(String[] args) throws Exception
        {
            JobConf conf = new JobConf(getConf(), getClass());
            conf.setJobName("Log Analyzer");

            FileInputFormat.addInputPath(conf, new Path(args[0]));
            FileOutputFormat.setOutputPath(conf, new Path(args[1]));

            conf.setOutputKeyClass(Text.class);
            conf.setOutputValueClass(IntWritable.class);

            conf.setMapperClass(LogMapper.class);
            conf.setCombinerClass(LogReducer.class);
            conf.setReducerClass(LogReducer.class);

            JobClient.runJob(conf);
            return 0;
        }

        public static void main(String[] args) throws Exception {
            int exitCode = ToolRunner.run(new LogAnalysisDriver(), args);
            System.exit(exitCode);
        }
}
```

To use the simple log analyzer, we must compile the driver, map, and reduce methods into a JAR file and load the JAR file into an S3 bucket. In the next sections, we'll run the methods built here against the sample log, and then run an Amazon EMR Job Flow to generate the log frequency analysis results.

Running an Amazon EMR Cluster

Let's walk through executing the simple log analyzer in Amazon EMR. Start by choosing Create Cluster from the Amazon EMR Console (*https://console.aws.amazon.com/*

elasticmapreduce/home). As shown in Figure 2-8, the Job Flow is given a name and the S3 location to use to write any log information from the Cluster, or Job Flow, run.

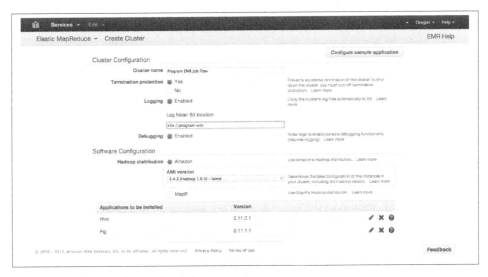

Figure 2-8. Amazon EMR New Cluster creation

Under Add Step, select the step type of Custom JAR. The parameters and location of our Custom JAR are defined for the step by selecting Configure and add. Our Custom JAR is added to the EMR Cluster by configuring a processing step in the Steps section. In defining the parameters for the job in Figure 2-9, we specify the JAR filename and location based on its location in S3 storage. We also define the parameters needed for the execution of the Job Flow as arguments. The first parameter is the main driver class in the JAR file. In Example 2-5, a set of required parameters defines the input file and output path of the results. The sample input file—_sample-syslog.log_—is set as the input file, and a new S3 location is defined as the output object to store the analysis from the Job Flow. Below the Step configuration is a setting to Auto-terminate the cluster after our step has completed. In the examples in this book, we will set this setting to yes so the EMR cluster will go away after it is finished processing. This can help to reduce the usage charges in AWS. Without setting this option, the cluster will continue running until you choose to terminate it from the EMR Console. You will continue to be charges AWS usage charges until the cluster terminates.

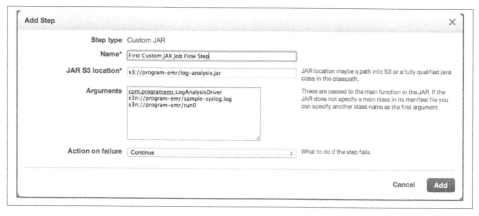

Figure 2-9. Amazon EMR Job Flow step parameters

For the remaining options in the Create Cluster screen, we will use the default sizing options to run the first Job Flow. At the end, as shown in Figure 2-10, the new Job Flow is created and your first Amazon EMR Job Flow is off and running in Amazon's data center!

Figure 2-10. Amazon running the Custom JAR in the EMR Console

A common cause of Job Flow failure is the use of an S3 output location that already exists. In the examples, we chose an output location that did not already exist in the S3 bucket prior to running the Job Flow. If the output path specified in the JAR parameters already exists, in most instances it will cause the job to fail. You may experience this by trying to run the same job more than once with the exact same parameters. The first time the Job Flow is run it will succeed, but if you run it again with exactly the same parameters, all subsequent attempts will fail.

Viewing Our Results

After the job completes, the analysis results will be available in S3 and you can retrieved them to review the frequency counts in the log. The job will generate a part file for each reducer task that is created by Amazon EMR. In general, a reducer is run on each of the core and task nodes in the Amazon EMR cluster. Looking at the results of one of these part files, we can see that they look very similar to what we expected from the walkthrough of the MapReduce process with pseudocode:

```
Apr 21 19:16:38  ❶   50 ❷
Apr 21 19:16:43     159
Apr 21 19:16:44     159
Apr 21 19:16:47     160
...
```

❶   The key selected in the mapper was the date and time of the log entry. The key was emitted out in the results by the reducer.

❷   The reducer counted the number of instances of each key, and the total is emitted as the second column of the result set.

The output from Amazon EMR may be one or many individual part files. The number of part files generated is related to the number of reduce processes executed in the Amazon EMR cluster. If your application calls for recombining the result set into a single consolidated file, you can accomplish this by taking the result set and loading it into an Amazon Relational Database (*http://aws.amazon.com/rds/*), or running the result set through another application or Amazon EMR Job Flow.

Debugging a Job Flow

You may be asking yourself now, "What will I do if I have an error in my application that is running in the cloud?" Fortunately, there are a number of tools and techniques available to find out more information about Amazon EMR jobs running in the cloud. In a time-honored tradition, let's add a number of print statements to the mapper and reducer methods so we can walk through some debugging techniques.

In the mapper method in Example 2-6, a standard error output line is added to detail that the application is executing the map method of the Job Flow.

Example 2-6. Mapper with logging statements

```java
import java.io.IOException;

import org.apache.hadoop.io.IntWritable;
import org.apache.hadoop.io.LongWritable;
import org.apache.hadoop.io.Text;
import org.apache.hadoop.mapred.MapReduceBase;
import org.apache.hadoop.mapred.Mapper;
import org.apache.hadoop.mapred.OutputCollector;
import org.apache.hadoop.mapred.Reporter;

public class LogMapper extends MapReduceBase
    implements Mapper<LongWritable, Text, Text, IntWritable>
{
    private Text word = new Text();
    private final static IntWritable one = new IntWritable( 1 );

    public void map( LongWritable key,
                     Text value,
                     OutputCollector<Text, IntWritable> output,
                     Reporter reporter) throws IOException
    {
        // Get the value as a String
        String text = value.toString();

        // Output a log message
        System.err.println("We are inside the map method"); ❶

        // Retrieve the date and time out of the log message, first 15 characters
        String SyslogDateTime = text.substring(0, 15);

        // Output the syslog date and time as the key and 1 as the value
        output.collect( new Text(SyslogDateTime), one );
    }
}
```

❶ A simple log statement to indicate the execution of the `map` routine in the log output

For the reduce method, we'll add similar logging to the routine to indicate the execution of the reducer. In addition, we'll intentionally introduce an arithmetic error to create a problem in the application—a division-by-zero operation will cause the reduce routine to fail during execution. Example 2-7 shows the changes made to the reduce method.

Example 2-7. Reducer that will fail with an arithmetic exception

```java
import java.io.IOException;
import java.util.Iterator;

import org.apache.hadoop.io.IntWritable;
import org.apache.hadoop.io.Text;
import org.apache.hadoop.mapred.MapReduceBase;
import org.apache.hadoop.mapred.OutputCollector;
import org.apache.hadoop.mapred.Reducer;
import org.apache.hadoop.mapred.Reporter;

public class LogReducer extends MapReduceBase
  implements Reducer<Text, IntWritable, Text, IntWritable>
{
    public void reduce( Text key, Iterator<IntWritable> values,
            OutputCollector<Text, IntWritable> output,
            Reporter reporter) throws IOException
    {
        // Output a log message
        System.err.println("We are inside the reduce method"); ❶

        // Counts the occurrences of the date and time
        int count = 0;
        while( values.hasNext() )
        {
            // Output a log message
            System.err.println("Uh oh!  We are going to divide by zero!");

                // Add the value to our count and divide by zero
                count += ( values.next().get() / 0 ); ❷
        }

        // Output the date and time with its count
        output.collect( key, new IntWritable( count ) );
    }
}
```

❶ A simple log statement to indicate execution of the reducer in the log output

❷ The alteration of the calculation to do divide by zero to cause the reducer to fail

Now that the application has been modified to intentionally fail, let's upload the new JAR file and run through a debug of the application in Amazon EMR.

Running Our Job Flow with Debugging

When creating a new Job Flow, we have the option to enable logging and debugging, and we can enable them independently. During the development phases of an application, it makes sense to enable these options to review application runs and track problems. When logging is enabled, the logs of each Job Flow are written to an S3 location that is chosen on Job Flow creation. If debugging is also enabled, Amazon EMR creates indexes of the logfiles' contents, which enables the Debug view of steps and tasks on the Amazon EMR Management Console to review a Job Flow run.

The same initial parameters used in Figures 2-8 and 2-9 are used to start the Job Flow. When setting up a new cluster, or Job Flow, in Figure 2-8 select a location to store the Job Flow logs. The debugging option is turned on by default, but confirm this option is enabled before starting the Job Flow.

The Job Flow happily gets started by Amazon EMR as before, but when the job finishes it does not show as `Terminated - All Steps Completed` as it did earlier. Reviewing the state of the Job Flow in the Amazon EMR console shows it as simply `Terminated`. Looking at the S3 output location, output from the failed run is not available in the *run0* folder.

 Enabling Job Flow logging and debugging is a great idea in development and testing. However, leaving logging and debugging turned on for production Job Flows can use up a significant amount of S3 storage for the logfile and SimpleDB indexes. These options may also greatly impact the performance of a Job Flow. Many developers will choose to use Amazon AWS libraries or third-party logging utilities to control and set logging levels for their Job Flows in production environments.

Reviewing Job Flow Log Structure

Each Job Flow in Amazon EMR is given a unique identifier. The Job Flow IDs follow the pattern of "j-XXXXXXXXXXXXX." In Figure 2-11, the Amazon EMR console gives a number of details about the execution of a Job Flow. By clicking on the Job Flow that terminated with errors in the EMR Management Console, details including the unique ID Amazon EMR assigned to the Job Flow are displayed in the `Cluster Details` page.

Figure 2-11. Job Flow name in the Amazon EMR console

Looking in the S3 bucket and path that were set as the log location on the Job Flow in Amazon EMR, we can see a number of new files and folders are now available following the Job Flow execution. The folder name has the same name as the unique Job Flow ID that Amazon assigned to it in the Amazon EMR console. The directory structure of the logs for the failed Job Flow run in the example from Figure 2-11 appears in a folder named *j-391947SOBCQM*. The following list describes the details of the directory structure and information recorded about the Job Flow run in S3, as well as the purpose of each recorded element:

daemons

The logs from each Hadoop process are stored in this folder. There is a directory for each EC2 instance that composed our Amazon EMR cluster. The directory name is the same name as the EC2 instance used in our cluster. You can determine the purpose of each node by reviewing the logfiles in each directory. Each node can be a data node or job tracker node, which map to the core, task, and master groups discussed earlier.

jobs

The configuration settings used during Job Flow execution in the Amazon EMR cluster are available in the logs in this folder. There are also independent logfiles that detail the reduce and map execution and the number of attempts performed on each of these.

node

Node logs detail the bootstrap actions taken on each node. The directory structure starts with the same name as the EC2 instance that composed the Amazon EMR cluster. The details of the logfiles contained here can be useful if you are using a number of custom bootstrap actions in the setup of your cluster.

steps

Job Flows are broken into steps. The example Job Flow in this chapter is a very simple process that only contains two steps: the startup, which is performed by Amazon EMR on every Job Flow, and the MapReduce phase that runs the map and reduce methods. On more complex Job Flows, there may be many step directories, or one for each step in the overall MapReduce Job Flow. The logs of each step have the following structure:

controller

Information about the execution of the step and the status of the step at the end of the execution.

syslog

Lists the execution of the step and the status of each task attempt. In our test, you can see each task attempt returned a "FAILED" status.

stdout

The standard output from the process run in the step.

stderr

The standard error from the process run in the step. Because the logging information was written to standard error in the map and reduce methods, the log information appears here in step 2 as well as the stack trace when the application performs a divide-by-zero operation.

task-attempts

The logs for each task attempt are stored here. The logs of each task have the following structure:

syslog

Detailed log information on the execution attempt of the task. In the recent run, a divide-by-zero exception appears in the logfile along with the stack trace of the failure to help trace the error to the line number in the code that failed.

stdout

The standard output from the process run of the attempt.

stderr

The standard error from the process run of the attempt. Because the logging information was written to standard error in the map and reduce methods, the individual log statements are visible in the output of the log information here for each attempt.

If debugging had not been enabled on the Job Flow, you'd need to review the logfiles individually to locate the application error. This is definitely possible, but because we did enable debugging, we can use the Amazon EMR console debug feature to review the logs without needing to understand the log hierarchy and execution process of the application.

Debug Through the Amazon EMR Console

When you review the Steps section of the Cluster Details page, you can see each step that was attempted and its status in the debug user interface in the EMR Console. From the previous section on logfiles, this information is stored in /jobid/steps and can also be viewed directly in S3. Figure 2-12 shows the graphical representation of the step log data in the Amazon EMR Console.

Figure 2-12. Amazon EMR Cluster Details displaying the log files and debugger actions of the failed Job Flow

Looking at each of the steps in the Cluster Details from Figure 2-12 shows that the execution of the Custom JAR application failed. The Custom JAR step represents the execution of the map and reduce methods on your syslog data. The controller, syslog, stderr, and stdout map directly to the log structure discussed earlier. The map and reduce methods written earlier write their log information to standard error with Java calls to System.err.println(). In reviewing the stderr logs from the example step named First Custom JAR Job Flow Step, the log output displays the exception being thrown by arithmetic error in the Job Flow in Figure 2-13 .

```
java.lang.ArithmeticException: / by zero
    at com.programemr.LogReducer.reduce(LogReducer.java:31)
    at com.programemr.LogReducer.reduce(LogReducer.java:13)
    at org.apache.hadoop.mapred.Task$OldCombinerRunner.combine(Task.java:1436)
    at org.apache.hadoop.mapred.MapTask$MapOutputBuffer.sortAndSpill(MapTask.java:1452)
    at org.apache.hadoop.mapred.MapTask$MapOutputBuffer.flush(MapTask.java:1314)
    at org.apache.hadoop.mapred.MapTask.runOldMapper(MapTask.java:443)
    at org.apache.hadoop.mapred.MapTask.run(MapTask.java:377)
    at org.apache.hadoop.mapred.Child$4.run(Child.java:255)
    at java.security.AccessController.doPrivileged(Native Method)
    at javax.security.auth.Subject.doAs(Subject.java:396)
    at org.apache.hadoop.security.UserGroupInformation.doAs(UserGroupInformation.java:1132)
    at org.apache.hadoop.mapred.Child.main(Child.java:249)

attempt_201306152031_0001_m_000000_0: We are inside the map method
attempt_201306152031_0001_m_000000_0: We are inside the map method
attempt_201306152031_0001_m_000000_0: We are inside the map method
attempt_201306152031_0001_m_000000_0: We are inside the map method
attempt_201306152031_0001_m_000000_0: We are inside the map method
attempt_201306152031_0001_m_000000_0: We are inside the map method
attempt_201306152031_0001_m_000000_0: We are inside the map method
attempt_201306152031_0001_m_000000_0: We are inside the map method
attempt_201306152031_0001_m_000000_0: We are inside the map method
attempt_201306152031_0001_m_000000_0: We are inside the map method
attempt_201306152031_0001_m_000000_0: We are inside the map method
attempt_201306152031_0001_m_000000_0: We are inside the map method
attempt_201306152031_0001_m_000000_0: We are inside the map method
attempt_201306152031_0001_m_000000_0: We are inside the map method
attempt_201306152031_0001_m_000000_0: We are inside the map method
attempt_201306152031_0001_m_000000_0: We are inside the map method
attempt_201306152031_0001_m_000000_0: We are inside the map method
attempt_201306152031_0001_m_000000_0: We are inside the map method
attempt_201306152031_0001_m_000000_0: We are inside the map method
attempt_201306152031_0001_m_000000_0: We are inside the map method
attempt_201306152031_0001_m_000000_0: We are inside the map method
attempt_201306152031_0001_m_000000_0: We are inside the map method
attempt_201306152031_0001_m_000000_0: We are inside the map method
attempt_201306152031_0001_m_000000_0: We are inside the map method
attempt_201306152031_0001_m_000000_0: We are inside the map method
attempt_201306152031_0001_m_000000_0: We are inside the map method
attempt_201306152031_0001_m_000000_0: We are inside the map method
attempt_201306152031_0001_m_000000_0: We are inside the map method
attempt_201306152031_0001_m_000000_0: We are inside the map method
```

Figure 2-13. Failed step logging output and exception

In this simple error case, this is probably enough information to help us pinpoint the problem in the application. In a real-world scenario, however, there may have been individual tasks in the Job Flow that failed due to data-specific issues. After clicking on the View Jobs option of the failed step, you see a graphical view with the job details for S3 located in the *jobs* folder of the logs.

Drilling further down into the run of the Job Flow, you can get a view of the individual tasks that composed the Job Flow by clicking on View Tasks. The task view in the debugger is sourced from the indexed information from the log data in the *jobs* folder. When you look at the raw log in Figure 2-14 and compare this to the graphical view in the Amazon EMR console in Figure 2-15, it becomes evident why some may prefer to use the graphical debugger for troubleshooting.

Meta VERSION="1" .
Job JOBID="job_201306152031_0001" JOBNAME="Log Analyzer" USER="hadoop" SUBMIT_TIME="1371328406172" .
JOBCONF="hdfs://10\.240\.123\.19:9000/mnt/var/lib/hadoop/tmp/mapred/hadoop/\.staging/job_201306152031_0001/job\.xml" VIEW_JOB="*" MODIFY_JOB="*"
JOB_QUEUE="default" .
Job JOBID="job_201306152031_0001" JOB_PRIORITY="NORMAL" .
Job JOBID="job_201306152031_0001" LAUNCH_TIME="1371328407896" TOTAL_MAPS="8" TOTAL_REDUCES="3" JOB_STATUS="PREP" .
Task TASKID="task_201306152031_0001_m_000009" TASK_TYPE="SETUP" START_TIME="1371328408659" SPLITS="" .
MapAttempt TASK_TYPE="SETUP" TASKID="task_201306152031_0001_m_000009" TASK_ATTEMPT_ID="attempt_201306152031_0001_m_000009_0" START_TIME="1371328410547" .
TRACKER_NAME="tracker_10\.193\.133\.142:localhost/127\.0\.0\.1:55568" HTTP_PORT="9103" .
MapAttempt TASK_TYPE="SETUP" TASKID="task_201306152031_0001_m_000009" TASK_ATTEMPT_ID="attempt_201306152031_0001_m_000009_0" TASK_STATUS="SUCCESS"
FINISH_TIME="1371328417115" HOSTNAME="/default-rack/10\.193\.133\.142" STATE_STRING="setup" COUNTERS="{(FileSystemCounters)(FileSystemCounters)[(FILE_BYTES_WRITTEN)
(FILE_BYTES_WRITTEN)(24662)]}{(org\.apache\.hadoop\.mapred.Task$Counter)(Map-Reduce Framework)[(PHYSICAL_MEMORY_BYTES)(Physical memory \\(bytes\\) snapshot)
(49451008)][(SPILLED_RECORDS)(Spilled Records)(0)][(CPU_MILLISECONDS)(CPU time spent \\(ms\\))(30)][(COMMITTED_HEAP_BYTES)(Total committed heap usage \\(bytes\\))
(16252928)][(VIRTUAL_MEMORY_BYTES)(Virtual memory \\(bytes\\) snapshot)(475250688)]}" .
MapAttempt TASK_TYPE="SETUP" TASK_STATUS="SUCCESS" FINISH_TIME="1371328417811" COUNTERS="{(FileSystemCounters)(FileSystemCounters)
[(FILE_BYTES_WRITTEN)(FILE_BYTES_WRITTEN)(24662)]}{(org\.apache\.hadoop\.mapred.Task$Counter)(Map-Reduce Framework)[(PHYSICAL_MEMORY_BYTES)(Physical memory \\
(bytes\\) snapshot)(49451008)][(SPILLED_RECORDS)(Spilled Records)(0)][(CPU_MILLISECONDS)(CPU time spent \\(ms\\))(30)][(COMMITTED_HEAP_BYTES)(Total committed heap
usage \\(bytes\\))(16252928)][(VIRTUAL_MEMORY_BYTES)(Virtual memory \\(bytes\\) snapshot)(475250688)]}" .
Job JOBID="job_201306152031_0001" JOB_STATUS="RUNNING" .
Task TASKID="task_201306152031_0001_m_000000" TASK_TYPE="MAP" START_TIME="1371328417817" SPLITS="/default-rack/localhost" .
Task TASKID="task_201306152031_0001_m_000001" TASK_TYPE="MAP" START_TIME="1371328417819" SPLITS="/default-rack/localhost" .
Task TASKID="task_201306152031_0001_m_000002" TASK_TYPE="MAP" START_TIME="1371328418049" SPLITS="/default-rack/localhost" .
Task TASKID="task_201306152031_0001_m_000003" TASK_TYPE="MAP" START_TIME="1371328418050" SPLITS="/default-rack/localhost" .
MapAttempt TASK_TYPE="MAP" TASKID="task_201306152031_0001_m_000000" TASK_ATTEMPT_ID="attempt_201306152031_0001_m_000000_0" START_TIME="1371328417860" .
TRACKER_NAME="tracker_10\.193\.133\.142:localhost/127\.0\.0\.1:55568" HTTP_PORT="9103" .
MapAttempt TASK_TYPE="MAP" TASKID="task_201306152031_0001_m_000000" TASK_ATTEMPT_ID="attempt_201306152031_0001_m_000000_0" TASK_STATUS="FAILED"
FINISH_TIME="1371328425939" HOSTNAME="10\.193\.133\.142" ERROR="java\.lang\.ArithmeticException: / by zero
        at com\.programmr\.LogReducer\.reduce(LogReducer\.java:31)
        at com\.programmr\.LogReducer\.reduce(LogReducer\.java:13)
        at org\.apache\.hadoop\.mapred\.Task$OldCombinerRunner\.combine(Task\.java:1436)
        at org\.apache\.hadoop\.mapred\.MapTask$MapOutputBuffer\.sortAndSpill(MapTask\.java:1452)
        at org\.apache\.hadoop\.mapred\.MapTask$MapOutputBuffer\.flush(MapTask\.java:1314)
        at org\.apache\.hadoop\.mapred\.MapTask\.runOldMapper(MapTask\.java:443)
        at org\.apache\.hadoop\.mapred\.MapTask\.run(MapTask\.java:377)
        at org\.apache\.hadoop\.mapred\.Child$4\.run(Child\.java:255)
        at java\.security\.AccessController\.doPrivileged(Native Method)
        at javax\.security\.auth\.Subject\.doAs(Subject\.java:396)
        at org\.apache\.hadoop\.security\.UserGroupInformation\.doAs(UserGroupInformation\.java:1132)
        at org\.apache\.hadoop\.mapred\.Child\.main(Child\.java:249)
" .
Task TASKID="task_201306152031_0001_m_000004" TASK_TYPE="MAP" START_TIME="1371328426905" SPLITS="/default-rack/localhost" .
MapAttempt TASK_TYPE="MAP" TASKID="task_201306152031_0001_m_000001" TASK_ATTEMPT_ID="attempt_201306152031_0001_m_000001_0" START_TIME="1371328417862" .
TRACKER_NAME="tracker_10\.193\.133\.142:localhost/127\.0\.0\.1:55568" HTTP_PORT="9103" .
MapAttempt TASK_TYPE="MAP" TASKID="task_201306152031_0001_m_000001" TASK_ATTEMPT_ID="attempt_201306152031_0001_m_000001_0" TASK_STATUS="FAILED"
FINISH_TIME="1371328431596" HOSTNAME="10\.193\.133\.142" ERROR="java\.lang\.ArithmeticException: / by zero
        at com\.programmr\.LogReducer\.reduce(LogReducer\.java:31)
        at com\.programmr\.LogReducer\.reduce(LogReducer\.java:13)
        at org\.apache\.hadoop\.mapred\.Task$OldCombinerRunner\.combine(Task\.java:1436)
        at org\.apache\.hadoop\.mapred\.MapTask$MapOutputBuffer\.sortAndSpill(MapTask\.java:1452)
        at org\.apache\.hadoop\.mapred\.MapTask$MapOutputBuffer\.flush(MapTask\.java:1314)

Figure 2-14. Raw job log data with task status

You can further drill down from the tasks in Figure 2-15 to view each attempt Amazon EMR made in trying to get the Job Flow to complete. When you click View Attempts, you'll see the familiar syslog, stderr, stdout structure from the log data under your *task-attempts* folder on S3 in graphical form.

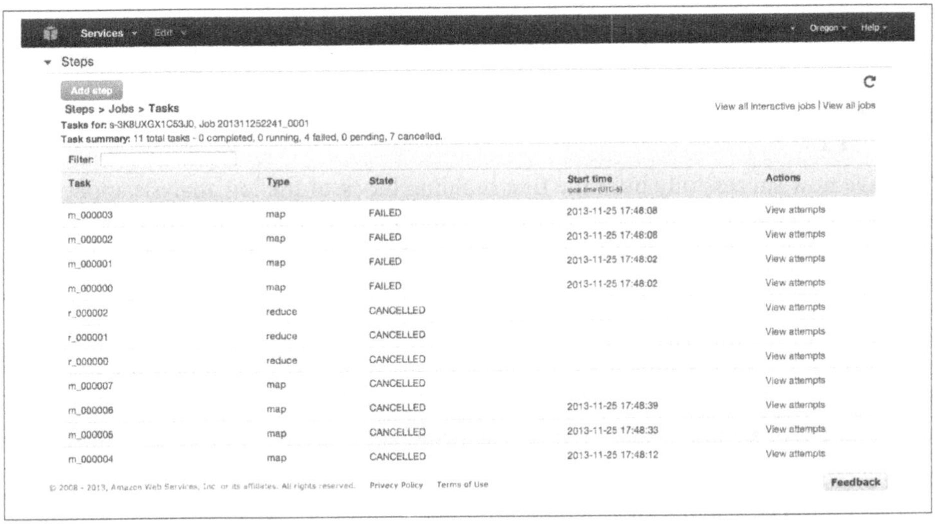

Figure 2-15. Task view in the Amazon EMR debugger in Cluster Details

Here you may be able to discover situations where the individual task attempts succeeded or failed if you had cases where different data situations are causing failure only occasionally. If you click stderr, you can see the individual log messages from the execution `map` and `reduce` methods from the Job Flow run:

```
...
We are inside the map method
We are inside the map method
We are inside the map method
We are inside the map method
We are inside the map method
We are inside the reduce method
Uh oh!  We are going to divide by zero!
```

The exception generated intentionally in the application is under syslog. Here the stack trace of the exception lists the call tree leading up to the error, and the error can be traced back to the line of code that caused it. You can find the same information tracing through the logs in S3, but the debugger in the Amazon EMR console allows you to conveniently drill down through the logs without needing to jump back and forth between different files in the S3 log structure.

```
...
2013-06-15 20:34:47,162 INFO org.apache.hadoop.io.compress.CodecPool (main): ...
2013-06-15 20:34:47,168 INFO org.apache.hadoop.mapred.TaskLogsTruncater ...
2013-06-15 20:34:47,250 INFO org.apache.hadoop.io.nativeio.NativeIO (main): ...
2013-06-15 20:34:47,250 INFO org.apache.hadoop.io.nativeio.NativeIO (main): ...
2013-06-15 20:34:47,253 WARN org.apache.hadoop.mapred.Child (main): Error ...
java.lang.ArithmeticException: / by zero
        at com.programemr.LogReducer.reduce(LogReducer.java:31)
            at com.programemr.LogReducer.reduce(LogReducer.java:13)
            at org.apache.hadoop.mapred.Task$OldCombinerRunner.combine(Task.java:1436)
```

Our Application and Real-World Uses

We have now successfully built the first building block of the log analysis application described in Chapter 1. The application can now receive syslog-formatted log records and determine the frequency of log events using Amazon EMR to count the number of records per second.

This application is primarily focused on log analysis, but counting and frequency analysis has many known uses in other data analysis situations. The MapReduce application is performing what is considered a *summarization* design pattern by simply summing up the values of a common key. Other real-world applications of this technique are:

Load or usage analysis
> Many times it is useful to know how many users access a server or a website throughout a time period. Web access logs or application logs that include the

timestamps of user events could be imported and processed with a similar Map-Reduce application to determine usage frequency.

Minimum, maximum, average, and trending

From the individual number of events per second we calculated in this chapter, you could load this data into a database, Excel, or even another Amazon EMR Job Flow and determine what the maximum, minimum, and average load of events were on the server throughout the day. This same technique could be used to determine the peak traffic to a website to know if more capacity should be purchased or planned, when to have more staff available throughout the day, or what may be common slow periods so you can schedule maintenance or reduce staffing.

CHAPTER 3

Data Filtering Design Patterns and Scheduling Work

Our initial example from the previous chapter was a fairly simple application, but by now you should understand the basics of getting an Amazon EMR job running with log data. The application only involved grouping data records based on time in order to determine the frequency of the messages we received every second. However, in many data analysis problems, you want to filter your data down to a smaller data set and focus the analysis on only key parts of the data set that are interesting. Like our log analysis scenario, a lot of the data analysis problems focus on analyzing error scenarios and anomalies. With large data sets this may feel like finding a needle in a haystack.

In this chapter, we'll extend the Amazon EMR application to demonstrate a number of additional useful MapReduce patterns for filtering and analyzing data sets. In demonstrating these new building blocks, we'll use a new data source that contains a greater variety of data than the earlier scenario. Going back to our NASA theme, you will use a web access log published by NASA (*http://ita.ee.lbl.gov/html/contrib/NASA-HTTP.html*) and analyze this log for web server errors. The MapReduce patterns that we'll look at will reduce the web server log data down to find requests resulting in HTTP errors on NASA's website. Additionally, we'll combine concepts learned in Chapters 2 and 3 to show how filtering and summarization can be used to gain greater insights into the data.

Toward the end of this chapter, we'll look at production aspects of Amazon EMR applications with a focus on some basic ways to schedule the data processing work with AWS services and tools. Companies that are heavy users of Amazon EMR sometimes build entire proprietary workflow systems to control, schedule, and maintain the AWS resources used by their organization. Netflix, for example, recently open-sourced its Genie (*http://techblog.netflix.com/2013/01/hadoop-platform-as-service-in-cloud.html*) system, which it is building to manage its Amazon EMR clusters, Job Flows, and scheduling. There are a number of great utilities already available at AWS, including the Amazon EMR command-line interface (CLI), that you can utilize to achieve a number of basic Amazon EMR operational tasks without needing to build an entire workflow system yourself. To that end, we'll do a basic walkthrough of using the Amazon EMR CLI with Unix scripts and utilities running inside an Amazon EC2 instance to demonstrate scheduling Job Flows in Amazon EMR.

In addition to the Amazon EMR CLI, this chapter will explore the use of the AWS Data Pipeline (*http://aws.amazon.com/datapipeline/*). The Data Pipeline allows you to create workflow processes to move data between AWS services, schedule work like Amazon EMR workflows for data analysis, and perform numerous other functions. We use it to build a scheduling scenario for the web log filtering Job Flow created in this chapter.

Extending the Application Example

The application components in this chapter will follow the same data flow pattern covered in Chapter 2. From Chapter 1, you will recall part of the example application pulled in a data set from a web server. Web server log data will be the input into the workflow where we'll extend the application components to do deeper analysis using MapReduce design patterns. Figure 3-1 shows the portion of our overall application and the flow of data through the system in this chapter.

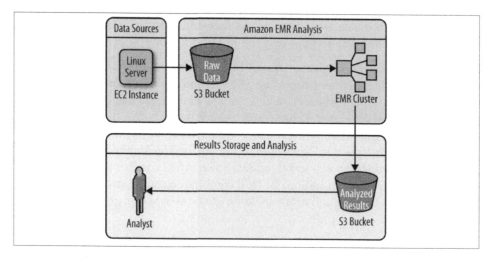

Figure 3-1. Chapter application data and workflow architecture

Understanding Web Server Logs

Web servers like Apache and IIS typically log every request that users and systems make to retrieve information from a web server. Many companies today are already using their web server logs for data analysis problems. The use of these logs ranges from A/B testing (*http://www.smashingmagazine.com/2010/06/24/the-ultimate-guide-to-a-b-testing/*) of new website designs to analyzing user website actions to improve sales.

NASA published the web server logfile used in this chapter back in 1995. At the time, these web access logs were used as part of a paper entitled "Web Server Workload Characterization: The Search for Invariants" (*http://dl.acm.org/citation.cfm?id=233034*) and appeared in the proceedings of the 1996 ACM SIGMETRICS Conference on the Measurement and Modeling of Computer Systems. This seems like a long time ago, but the format and meaning of the web server logs has not changed greatly over the years.

You can download the logs to use in the Amazon EMR MapReduce building blocks developed throughout this chapter. We'll perform the analysis using the July 1995 logfile (*ftp://ita.ee.lbl.gov/traces/NASA_access_log_Jul95.gz*). The logfile has a good variety and diversity of successful and unsuccessful web requests made to the web server.

After downloading the web access log and opening the file, looking at the individual log records will give us a number of entries similar to the following:

```
piweba2y.prodigy.com - - [02/Jul/1995:00:01:28 -0400] "GET ..." 404 -
dd04-014.compuserve.com - - [02/Jul/1995:00:01:28 -0400] "GET ..." 200 7074
j10.ptl5.jaring.my - - [02/Jul/1995:00:01:28 -0400] "GET ..." 304 0
198.104.162.38 - - [02/Jul/1995:00:01:28 -0400] "GET ..." 200 11853
buckbrgr.inmind.com - - [02/Jul/1995:00:01:29 -0400] "GET ..." 304 0
gilbert.nih.go.jp - - [02/Jul/1995:00:01:29 -0400] "GET ..." 200 1204
```

Individual log entries follow a pretty simple format of space-delimited columns, with quotes and brackets used to further delimit columns that contain spaces in the data. Let's first examine the meaning of each of these data elements. Looking at the data this way will help you figure out the `map` and `reduce` procedures to parse and analyze the web server log.

You won't use every column in the log in this chapter, but the data still needs to be parsed to get to the columns used in the analysis. A single log record row breaks down into the following data elements:

```
piweba2y.prodigy.com - - [02/Jul/1995:00:01:28 -0400]
    "GET /KSC.HTML HTTP/1.0" 404 -
```

IP address or hostname of client: -`piweba2y.prodigy.com`
   The first element is the IP address or hostname of the client computer making a request to retrieve information from the web server. In this dated example, note that the request came from some web client inside the Prodigy network.

Identity check directive: -
   This element is part of the identity check directive based on RFC 1413 (*http://www.ietf.org/rfc/rfc1413.txt*). In practice this data is very unreliable except in very tightly controlled networks. In the web logfile, a hyphen indicates that data is not available for this column. A common data analysis problem is having data sets with

missing or invalid data values. You can use filtering to remove data with these issues to cleanse the data prior to further analysis. For now, you don't have to worry about it, because we won't be focusing on this column for this chapter.

User ID: -

The third column is the user ID of the user making the request to the web server. This typically requires that you enable HTTP authentication to receive this information in the log. In this example record, no data is provided for this column and a hyphen indicates the empty value received.

Date, time, and time zone: `[02/Jul/1995:00:01:28 -0400]`

The fourth column is the date, time, and time zone offset of when the request completed on the web server. The time zone offset of (-0400) indicates the server is four hours behind coordinated universal time (UTC). UTC is a time similar to Greenwich Mean Time (GMT), but is not adjusted for daylight savings time. The incorporation of the time zone offset can help coordinate events across servers located in different time zones. The full date and time is enclosed in brackets (`[ ]`) so we can parse the data can be parsed utilizing the delimiters to retrieve the full time field, including any spaces in the data.

Web request: `"GET /KSC.HTML HTTP/1.0"`

The request line received from the client is delimited by double quotes. There is a lot of useful information in the request line—including if it was a `GET`, `PUT`, or other type of request—and, of course, the path and resource being requested. In this example, the client did a `GET` request for *KSC.HTML*. This column will be used in later examples to show the requests being made that resulted in an error in the web log.

HTTP status sode: `404`

This is the status code that the web server sent back to the client from the request. We'll use this later to filter out only web server records that contain requests that resulted in an error. The `map` procedure, shown later, will use this data to determine what data should be kept and what data should be thrown away. In general, the first digit of the status code designates the class of response from the web server. A successful response code has a beginning digit of 2; a redirection begins with a 3; an error caused by the web client begins with a 4; and an error on the web server begins with a 5. The full list of status codes is defined in the HTTP specification in RFC2616 (*http://www.ietf.org/rfc/rfc2616.txt*). In this example record, a 404 response code was sent back to the client. This means the request was for something that could be found on the web server. Isolating 404 requests could be useful in finding broken links in a website or potentially locating someone maliciously making lots of requests to find known scripts or command files that may help him gain access to a system.

Data size: -

The final data element is the size of the object returned. This is typically expressed in bytes transferred back to the client. The example record has a hyphen for the size of the data returned because the request was invalid and no object was found to return.

Now that the layout and meaning of the new data set has been covered, let's look at how data filtering can be done in an Amazon EMR application.

Finding Errors in the Web Logs Using Data Filtering

Data filtering is probably one of the simplest uses of the MapReduce framework. Filtering allows you to reduce your data set from a very large one to only a subset of data on whic you can do further processing. The filtered data set that is returned could be large or small—however, the key is the data has been filtered to support the application's analytics.

The MapReduce framework and Amazon EMR are well suited for performing a distributed filtering task. Amazon EMR splits the web log into a number of smaller data files depending on the number of core and task nodes in your cluster. The filtering process takes each smaller file and executes the `map` procedure of the Job Flow. The `map` procedure reduces the data set to the portions of the data needed for further analytics. Figure 3-2 shows a high-level diagram of how this process works and the MapReduce filter pattern that will be implemented in this chapter.

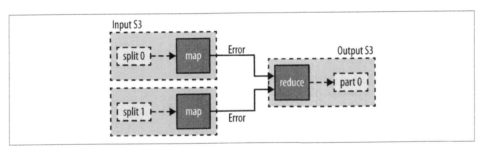

Figure 3-2. MapReduce filter pattern for error filtering

The following pseudocode demonstrates the algorithm being implemented in the mapper method:

```
map( "Log Record" )
    Parse Log Record elements
    If a record contains an error
      Emit Log Record and Error Code
    Else
      Do Nothing
```

In this case, the map procedure only emits the records that contain an HTTP status code that indicates an error occurred in the request. If the log entry is a successful request, the record will not be emitted from the mapper for any further analysis and processing. This has the effect of throwing away all the successful web requests and only passing along the error entries to the reduce phase of the Job Flow.

For many filtering scenarios, the reduce phase may not be necessary because the map portion of the code has already done the hard work of parsing the record and filtering down the data set. Thus, the pseudocode for our reducer is very simple:

```
reduce( Key, Values )
  for each value
    emit (Key)
```

The reduce phase of the Job Flow simply removes any grouping on keys of the data received from the earlier phases of the MapReduce cycle. The original error log line is emitted back out into the final result set. The results will show up as individual part files in an S3 bucket. The number of individual part files created is based on the number of core and task nodes that run the reduce procedure in the Amazon EMR Job Flow.

Now that the web server log format and the MapReduce filter pattern concepts have been covered, let's explore the actual map and reduce code needed to implement the web log filter.

Mapper Code

The mapper code looks like this:

```java
import java.io.IOException;
import java.util.regex.Matcher;
import java.util.regex.Pattern;

import org.apache.hadoop.io.IntWritable;
import org.apache.hadoop.io.LongWritable;
import org.apache.hadoop.io.Text;
import org.apache.hadoop.mapred.MapReduceBase;
import org.apache.hadoop.mapred.Mapper;
import org.apache.hadoop.mapred.OutputCollector;
import org.apache.hadoop.mapred.Reporter;

public class WebLogErrorFilterMapper extends MapReduceBase
implements Mapper<LongWritable, Text, Text, IntWritable>
{

    /** The number of fields that must be found. */
    public static final int NUM_FIELDS = 7;

    public void map( LongWritable key, // Offset into the file
                    Text value,
                    OutputCollector<Text, IntWritable> output,
```

```
                    Reporter reporter) throws IOException
{
    // Regular expression to parse Apache Web Log
    String logEntryPattern = "^(\\S+) (\\S+) (\\S+)
        \\[([\\w:/]+\\s[+\\-]\\d{4})\\]" + " \"(.+?)\" (\\d{3}) (\\S+)";

    // Get the Apache Web Log record as a String
        String logEntryLine = value.toString();

    // Compile regular expression for parsing input
    Pattern p = Pattern.compile(logEntryPattern);
    Matcher matcher = p.matcher(logEntryLine);

    // Validate we have a valid log record
    if (!matcher.matches() ||
                NUM_FIELDS != matcher.groupCount())
    {
        System.err.println("Bad log entry:");
        System.err.println(logEntryLine);
        return;
    }

        // Get the HTTP request information from the log entry
        Integer httpCode = Integer.parseInt(matcher.group(6));

    // Filter any web requests that had a 300 HTTP return code or higher
    if ( httpCode >= 300 )
    {
            // Output the log line as the key and HTTP status as the value
        output.collect( value, new IntWritable(httpCode) );
    }
    }
}
```

A regular expression parses the individual data elements from each log record. The map procedure examines the HTTP status code from the parsed data and will only emit records out of the map method for an HTTP status code of 300 or greater. The results in the Job Flow processing only page requests that resulted in a redirect (300—399 status codes), a client error (400—499 status codes), or a server error (500—599 status codes). The filtering is performed in parallel, as the filtering work is distributed across the individual nodes in the Amazon EMR cluster.

Reducer Code

The reducer is very simple because the data set has already been filtered down in the mapper:

```
import java.io.IOException;
import java.util.Iterator;

import org.apache.hadoop.io.IntWritable;
```

```
import org.apache.hadoop.io.Text;
import org.apache.hadoop.mapred.MapReduceBase;
import org.apache.hadoop.mapred.OutputCollector;
import org.apache.hadoop.mapred.Reducer;
import org.apache.hadoop.mapred.Reporter;

public class WebLogErrorFilterReducer extends MapReduceBase
  implements Reducer<Text, IntWritable, Text, IntWritable>
{
    public void reduce( Text key, Iterator<IntWritable> values,
            OutputCollector<Text, IntWritable> output,
            Reporter reporter) throws IOException
    {
        // Iterate over all of the values and emit each key value pair
        while( values.hasNext() )
        {
            output.collect( key, new IntWritable( values.next().get() ) );
        }
    }
}
```

A simple loop through each value in the array passed to the reducer will emit each key and value pair into the final output data set. The reduce portion is not a requirement in MapReduce and could be eliminated from this filtering Job Flow. The reduce procedure is included in the application for completeness and to remove any unlikely grouping that could occur if duplicate log record entries were encountered by the mapper.

Driver Code

The driver code does not look very different from the work done in Chapter 2. The driver is required to set the map and reduce procedures in the Job Flow. The driver, as was implemented earlier, accepts the S3 input and output locations as arguments and sets the individual map and reduce class links to set up the running of the Job Flow.

```
import org.apache.hadoop.conf.Configured;
import org.apache.hadoop.fs.Path;
import org.apache.hadoop.io.IntWritable;
import org.apache.hadoop.io.Text;
import org.apache.hadoop.mapred.FileInputFormat;
import org.apache.hadoop.mapred.FileOutputFormat;
import org.apache.hadoop.mapred.JobClient;
import org.apache.hadoop.mapred.JobConf;
import org.apache.hadoop.util.Tool;
import org.apache.hadoop.util.ToolRunner;

import com.programemr.weblog_top_ten.WebLogErrorFilterMapper;
import com.programemr.weblog_top_ten.WebLogErrorFilterReducer;

public class WebLogDriver extends Configured implements Tool {
```

```
public int run(String[] args) throws Exception
{
    JobConf conf = new JobConf(getConf(), getClass());
    conf.setJobName("Web Log Analyzer");

    FileInputFormat.addInputPath(conf, new Path(args[0]));
    FileOutputFormat.setOutputPath(conf, new Path(args[1]));

    conf.setOutputKeyClass(Text.class);
    conf.setOutputValueClass(IntWritable.class);

    conf.setMapperClass(WebLogErrorFilterMapper.class);
    conf.setCombinerClass(WebLogErrorFilterReducer.class);
    conf.setReducerClass(WebLogErrorFilterReducer.class);

    JobClient.runJob(conf);
    return 0;
}

public static void main(String[] args) throws Exception {
    int exitCode = ToolRunner.run(new WebLogDriver(), args);
    System.exit(exitCode);
}

}
```

Running the MapReduce Filter Job

The process of running the filter Job Flow is nearly identical to the steps followed in
Chapter 2. Once the compiled Java JAR and the NASA Web Log have been uploaded to
an S3 bucket, you can create a new Cluster, or Job Flow, utilizing the "Create cluster"
option from the Amazon EMR Management Console (*https://console.aws.amazon.com/
elasticmapreduce/home*). The Job Flow takes parameters similar to those laid out in
Figure 3-3. The parameter for the new MapReduce JAR sets the main Java class along
with the input and output locations needed for starting the Job Flow processing.

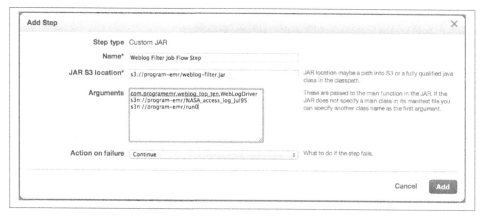

Figure 3-3. Example Amazon EMR filter Job Flow step parameters

Analyzing the Results

After the Job Flow completes, you can retrieve the results from the output S3 location specified in the Job Flow parameters. The original data set contained a number of successful and failed requests, and in the end, the final data set shows the filtering that occurred and a set of results that only contains the individual error lines.

The data flow through the Map and Reduce phases can be diagrammed like the pipeline in Figure 3-4.

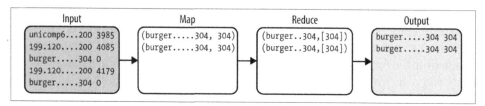

Figure 3-4. MapReduce Filter logical data flow

Let's walk through what occurred in the filter Job Flow using a snapshot of some of the sample data from the NASA web logfile. The following snapshot is truncated to improve readability:

```
unicomp6.unicomp.net - - [01/Jul/1995:00:00:06 -0400] "GET ..." 200 3985
199.120.110.21 - - [01/Jul/1995:00:00:09 -0400] "GET ..." 200 4085
burger.letters.com - - [01/Jul/1995:00:00:11 -0400] "GET ..." 304 0
199.120.110.21 - - [01/Jul/1995:00:00:11 -0400] "GET ..." 200 4179
burger.letters.com - - [01/Jul/1995:00:00:12 -0400] "GET ..." 304 0
burger.letters.com - - [01/Jul/1995:00:00:12 -0400] "GET ..." 200 0
205.212.115.106 - - [01/Jul/1995:00:00:12 -0400] "GET ..." 200 3985
```

The mapper method parsed each field and examined the HTTP status code value, only emitting lines that have a status code greater than 300. The entire original log line is passed as the key, and the HTTP status code that was examined by the mapper is the value. The HTTP status code emission enhances the readability of our final output because it will be placed as the last item on each output record. The output from the mapper would be similar to the following:

```
( burger.letters.com - - [01/Jul/1995:00:00:11 -0400] "GET ..." 304 0, 304 )
( burger.letters.com - - [01/Jul/1995:00:00:12 -0400] "GET ..." 304 0, 304 )
```

The data is further sorted and grouped by the MapReduce framework, and the re duce method will receive a set of grouped values. The log lines look the same with truncated GET request lines, but the individual requests are different. There are not any duplicate full log lines in the logfile, so the grouping that occurs after the mapper does not reduce the data set.

```
( burger.letters.com - - [01/Jul/1995:00:00:11 -0400] "GET ..." 304 0, [304] )
( burger.letters.com - - [01/Jul/1995:00:00:12 -0400] "GET ..." 304 0, [304] )
```

The simple reduce walks through the array of values in a loop and emits out each line and the HTTP status code. The final filtered results from the sample are shown here:

```
burger.letters.com - - [01/Jul/1995:00:00:11 -0400] "GET ..." 304 0    304
burger.letters.com - - [01/Jul/1995:00:00:12 -0400] "GET ..." 304 0    304
```

Building Summary Counts in Data Sets

We have now performed two basic but very common tasks in analyzing data. In many data analysis applications, key portions of a data set are chosen via filtering and then further calculations on this smaller set of data are performed. The counting example from Chapter 2 is an example of further analysis that could be done. In the log analysis application being used in this book, we can use a combination of these two analysis techniques to derive counts on the website URL locations in the NASA logs that resulted in an error. The code we'll show in the next section demonstrates how to combine these techniques.

Mapper Code

The incoming data is parsed into individual fields with the same regular expression as was done in "Mapper Code" on page 48. This time, though, the focus is on the HTTP request to specific web pages:

```
import java.io.IOException;
import java.util.regex.Matcher;
import java.util.regex.Pattern;

import org.apache.hadoop.io.IntWritable;
import org.apache.hadoop.io.LongWritable;
```

```java
import org.apache.hadoop.io.Text;
import org.apache.hadoop.mapred.MapReduceBase;
import org.apache.hadoop.mapred.Mapper;
import org.apache.hadoop.mapred.OutputCollector;
import org.apache.hadoop.mapred.Reporter;

public class WebLogErrorCountMapper extends MapReduceBase
implements Mapper<LongWritable, Text, Text, IntWritable>
{

private final static IntWritable one = new IntWritable( 1 );

/** The number of fields that must be found. */
public static final int NUM_FIELDS = 7;

public void map( LongWritable key, // Offset into the file
                 Text value,
                 OutputCollector<Text, IntWritable> output,
                 Reporter reporter) throws IOException
    {

        // Regular expression to parse Apache Web Log
        String logEntryPattern = "^(\\S+) (\\S+) (\\S+)
            \\[([\\w:/]+\\s[+\\-]\\d{4})\\]" + " \"(.+?)\" (\\d{3}) (\\S+)";

                // Get the Apache Web Log record as a String
        String logEntryLine = value.toString();

        // Compile regular expression for parsing input
        Pattern p = Pattern.compile(logEntryPattern);
        Matcher matcher = p.matcher(logEntryLine);

        // Validate we have a valid log record
        if (!matcher.matches() ||
                    NUM_FIELDS != matcher.groupCount())
        {
                    System.err.println("Bad log entry:");
                    System.err.println(logEntryLine);
                    return;
        }

                // Get the HTTP request information from the log entry
        Integer httpCode = Integer.parseInt(matcher.group(6));
        Text httpRequest = new Text(matcher.group(5));


        // Filter any web requests that had a 300 HTTP return code or higher
        if ( httpCode >= 300 )
        {
            // Output the HTTP Error code and page requested and 1 as the value
            //  We will use the value in the reducer to sum the total occurrences
            //   of the same web request and error returned from the server.
```

```
            output.collect( new Text(httpRequest), one );
        }
    }
}
```

The logic in the mapper pulls the HTTP status code and the HTTP request from the individual log entry. The emitted records from the map method select the entries with an HTTP status code of 300 or greater. This time, the key will be the HTTP request made, and we'll assign it a numerical value of 1 so a summation can be performed to total up the number of identical web requests.

Reducer Code

The reducer takes on the form of the summarization pattern used in Example 2-4. This is the same counting scenario used to find the frequency of log messages. The difference now is that the keys being delivered from the mapper method are a filtered set of web request errors instead of full log lines. The reducer will generate a total in the final result rather than ungrouping the data.

```
import java.io.IOException;
import java.util.Iterator;

import org.apache.hadoop.io.IntWritable;
import org.apache.hadoop.io.Text;
import org.apache.hadoop.mapred.MapReduceBase;
import org.apache.hadoop.mapred.OutputCollector;
import org.apache.hadoop.mapred.Reducer;
import org.apache.hadoop.mapred.Reporter;

public class WebLogErrorCountReducer extends MapReduceBase
    implements Reducer<Text, IntWritable, Text, IntWritable>
{
    public void reduce( Text key, Iterator<IntWritable> values,
            OutputCollector<Text, IntWritable> output,
            Reporter reporter) throws IOException
    {
        // Iterate over all of the values (counts of occurrences
        //     of the web requests)
        int count = 0;
        while( values.hasNext() )
        {
                // Add the value to our count
                count += values.next().get();
        }

        // Output the web request with its count (wrapped in an IntWritable)
        output.collect( key, new IntWritable( count ) );
    }
}
```

The driver code can be reused from our previous example in "Mapper Code" on page 53.

Analyzing the Filtered Counts Job

Recall the original data set that contained successful and failed requests. In this case, a similar filtering will reduce the data set for summarization in the reduce method. Let's walk through a sample of the data set again to review what is occurring in each of the methods with the combination of summarization and filtering. The new sample data set contains a number of rows like the following:

```
netcom16 ... "GET /icons/sound.xbm HTTP/1.0"
    200 530
alcott2 ... "GET /shuttle/missions/sts-71/images/KSC-95EC-0868.jpg HTTP/1.0"
    200 61848
www-b6 ... "GET /:/spacelink.msfc.nasa.gov HTTP/1.0" 404 -
sac1-109 ... "GET /shuttle/missions/sts-71/mission-sts-71.html HTTP/1.0"
    200 12040
jfpenter ... "GET /images/launch-logo.gif HTTP/1.0" 200 1713
ts02-ind-27 ... "GET /shuttle/countdown/video/livevideo.gif HTTP/1.0" 200 67065
sac1-109 ... "GET /shuttle/missions/sts-71/sts-71-patch-small.gif HTTP/1.0"
    200 12054
```

In the revised mapper method, each field is parsed and examined. The HTTP access request is emitted only with a status code greater than 300. The HTTP request field itself is used as the key, and you count the value of one to find out how many times the same request resulted in an error. The output of the mapper on the input file would then be similar to the following:

```
...
( "GET /:/spacelink.msfc.nasa.gov HTTP/1.0", 1 )
( "GET /:/spacelink.msfc.nasa.gov HTTP/1.0", 1 )
( "GET /:/spacelink.msfc.nasa.gov HTTP/1.0", 1 )
( "GET /:/spacelink.msfc.nasa.gov HTTP/1.0", 1 )
...
```

The data goes through the usual sorting and grouping by the MapReduce framework, and the reduce method receives a set of grouped values. A number of requests resulted in errors repeatedly in the data set, and they are grouped accordingly by the HTTP request key. The data set going to the reducer is grouped like the following example:

```
...
( "GET /%20%20history/apollo/apollo-13/apollo-13.html HTTP/1.0", [1] )
( "GET /%20history/apollo/apollo-13/apollo-13.html HTTP/1.0", [1, 1, 1, 1] )
( "GET /:/spacelink.msfc.nasa.gov HTTP/1.0", [1, 1, 1, 1, ...] )
( "GET /%3A/spacelink.msfc.nasa.gov HTTP/1.0", [1, 1, 1, 1, ...] )
( "GET /%7Eadverts/ibm/ad1/banner.gif HTTP/1.0", [1] )
...
```

The reduce method walks through the grouping that has been done from the mapper phase and adds up each value in the array. Because each of our keys is a request made to the web server and the value is simply the count of 1 for each occurrence, this has the net effect of creating a total count for each unique HTTP request that resulted in an error. The filter result set in the end is like this:

```
....
GET /%20%20history/apollo/apollo-13/apollo-13.html HTTP/1.0     1
GET /%20history/apollo/apollo-13/apollo-13.html HTTP/1.0        4
GET /%3A//spacelink.msfc.nasa.gov HTTP/1.0         31
GET /%3A/spacelink.msfc.nasa.gov HTTP/1.0          36
GET /%7Eadverts/ibm/ad1/banner.gif HTTP/1.0        1
....
```

> This book focuses primarily on the use of AWS and Amazon EMR to help you learn more about how you can build your application in Amazon's cloud. However, a solid understanding of MapReduce and software development patterns is a good foundation to start with before building an application of your own. To that end, we recommend *MapReduce Design Patterns: Building Effective Algorithms and Analytics for Hadoop and Other Systems (http://shop.oreilly.com/prod uct/0636920025122.do)* (O'Reilly) by Donald Miner and Adam Shook —it's an excellent resource to learn more about MapReduce patterns that could be relevant to any MapReduce project you start.

Job Flow Scheduling

Most of the items covered in the earlier chapters revolved around creating one-time runs of Job Flows. In a real-world operational scenario, the application will likely need to be a Job Flow that is run on a scheduled basis that processes new data when it becomes available.

The real strength of MapReduce and Amazon EMR is the ability to process large volumes of data. However, data may not always be available, or the time needed to load all required data into the cloud may necessitate processing the data in bulk on an hourly, daily, or weekly basis. This can also help to control the costs of running your Amazon EMR cluster.

The Amazon EMR Management Console allows new Job Flows to be created manually for one-time execution or long-running clusters. However, it does not have a scheduling option available. There are currently two major options available from Amazon. The Amazon EMR CLI can be used to control existing Job Flows and create new ones, or Amazon Data Pipeline can be used to create and schedule a full workflow of AWS services including Amazon EMR Job Flows.

Scheduling with the CLI

You can download the Amazon Elastic MapReduce Ruby client utility (Amazon EMR CLI) from Amazon's Developer Tools site (*http://aws.amazon.com/developertools/ 2264*). The utility can be run from anywhere, including other running EC2 instances you may already have provisioned in AWS. If you decide to run the utility on an EC2 instance, the Ruby programming language prerequisite is preloaded for you. However, the Amazon EMR CLI tool itself is not preloaded on the Amazon Machine Images (AMI), so you will need to upload and configure it to your running EC2 instance.

The Amazon EMR CLI provides a number of useful features as well as a number of features that are not directly available from the Amazon EMR Management Console. This section will focus on new Job Flow creation, but you may find each of the following options useful in the operation and control of Job Flows. Many of these options are available in Amazon's AWS API (*http://aws.amazon.com/sdkforjava/*), but you can perform them using this utility without needing to be a programmer.

Create a new Job Flow: `--create`
> This option allows you to create a new Job Flow from the command line, performing the same function as selecting Create New Job Flow in the Amazon EMR Management Console.

Create a Job Flow that stays running: `--alive`
> The `alive` option allows your Amazon EMR cluster to continue running after it has completed all the steps in a Job Flow. This option is available under the Advanced Options and is called Keep Alive when you are creating a Job Flow from the Console. This may be a useful feature if you want to add work, also known as *steps*, to an already running Amazon EMR cluster. You will need to specifically terminate the Job Flow if this option is used. You can terminate Job Flows from the Management Console or by using the Terminate option from the Amazon EMR CLI.

Resize a running Job Flow: `--modify-instance-group, --add-instance-group`
> When a new Job Flow is created from the Amazon EMR console, there is no way to change it or resize it from the user interface. If the initial Job Flow is too small and is taking too long to complete, the only option from the Management Console is to terminate it and restart the work. You can add task nodes using the `--add-instance-group` option or additional nodes to any of the group types in the Amazon EMR cluster using the `--modify-instance-group` option. Technically, the `--modify-instance-group` option allows an EMR cluster to be increased or decreased in size, but decreasing the number of Core or Master nodes from a running Job Flow can lead to data loss and cause the Job Flow to fail.

Adding JAR steps to Job Flows: `--jar, --main-class`

These options are used on Job Flow creation, but can also be used to add steps to an already running Job Flow. This can be useful when the `--alive` option is used on Job Flow creation and additional work needs to be added to an already running Amazon EMR cluster. The ability to add additional steps is not available from the Amazon EMR Management Console. The `--jar` and `--main-class` options are used for custom JAR MapReduce applications like the Job Flows demonstrated so far in this book. There are other corresponding command-line options if other Job Flow types are used.

Copying and retrieving files directly: `--put, --get`

The `--put` and `--get` options allow direct interaction with files on the Amazon EMR master node. If an application wants to bypass S3 and place work directly on the cluster, retrieve results, or do any custom functionality on the cluster directly, these options may be useful. In this book, we stick to the out-of-the-box functionality available in S3 and Amazon EMR rather than direct manipulation of the cluster.

Amazon is trying to combine a number of its AWS command line-utilities under a single AWS command-line interface (*http://aws.amazon.com/cli/*). This utility will allow you to use a single command-line utility to control many of the services you use at Amazon. Another great benefit of this utility is that it comes preloaded on the EC2 AMI and simply needs to be configured on any running EC2 instances. At the time of writing, the AWS command-line interface was released as a developer preview and was not mature enough for inclusion.

In the process of demonstrating Job Flow creation we will focus on the Amazon EMR CLI `--create` option. The examples will mimic similar creation and execution processes that were done manually in the Management Console in earlier chapters. Let's walk through a simple example of scheduling the MapReduce application from this chapter with cron and the Amazon EMR CLI.

To start, you need to create a script to start a new Job Flow. The script will be the input to a Unix cron schedule as shown here:

```
#!/bin/bash

~/elastic-mapreduce --create \
        --name "Filter Example Flow" \
        --num-instances 3 \ ❶
        --instance-type m1.small \ ❷
        --jar s3n://program-emr/weblog-filter.jar \ ❸
        --arg com.programemr.weblog_top_ten.WebLogDriver \ ❹
```

```
--arg s3n://program-emr/NASA_access_log_Jul95 \
--arg s3n://program-emr/run0
```

❶ Specifies the number of EC2 instances to use in an Amazon EMR cluster similar
    to manual runs in the Amazon EMR Management Console. These are broken
    out into master and core groups for the cluster.

❷ The type of EC2 instances to use for the Job Flow.

❸ The custom JAR file to use for the Job Flow.

❹ The list of arguments used in our previous examples to specify the main driver
    class, and the input and output S3 locations.

Let's run the script manually first and see what happens. You should see output from
the script similar to the following:

```
[ec2-user@ip-10-1-1-1 ~]$ ./ScheduleJobFlow.sh
Created job flow j-18EXVE5FLOWH1
[ec2-user@ip-10-1-1-1 ~]$
```

The script was saved on the EC2 instance with the name *ScheduleFlow.sh*.

The Job Flow starts and will appear in the Amazon EMR Management Console just like
the Job Flow executions that were done earlier. The Amazon EMR CLI outputs the
internal ID of the Job Flow created. We can use this later to review log output in S3 and
to terminate the Job Flow using the Amazon EMR CLI Terminate option.

To schedule the Job Flow to run every hour, you can configure cron to execute the script.
Cron is a Linux utility that is already part of the EC2 instance and most Unix and Linux
systems. This book will not go into all the details of cron, but *Linux Desktop Hacks: Tips
& Tools for Customizing and Optimizing your OS (http://shop.oreilly.com/product/
9780596009113.do)*, by Nicholas Petreley and Jono Bacon (O'Reilly), covers many of
the basics for automating scripts.

Following is a simple example of a crontab entry for scheduling the script at the beginning of the hour. This entry can be added to the file */etc/crontab* to schedule the script
with the cron daemon:

```
0 * * * * /user/ec2-user/ScheduleJobFlow.sh
```

The Job Flow will now be started every hour and will run to completion similar to earlier
manual executions performed from the Amazon EMR Management Console. We've
now automated the manual Job Flow creation from earlier with minimal scripting and
the use of cron as a scheduler.

Scheduling with AWS Data Pipeline

Automation gets much more complicated in scenarios that involve the coordination of actions on multiple AWS services, S3 object manipulation, and reattempting processes on failures. A more real-world scenario for a Job Flow is outlined in Figure 3-5.

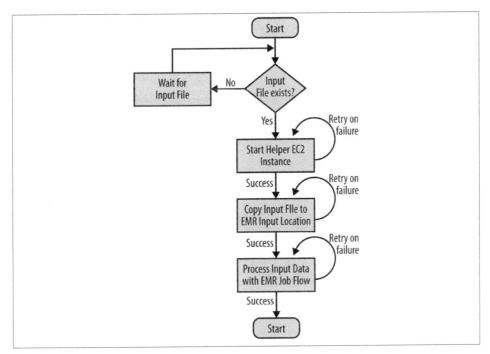

Figure 3-5. Job Flow automation with multiple services and dependencies

Prior to AWS Data Pipeline, accomplishing many of the items in this scenario required you to write numerous scripts, AWS utilities, and additional new applications using the AWS SDK (*http://aws.amazon.com/sdkforjava/*). With the release of AWS Data Pipeline, you can achieve this workflow using this single web service from Amazon.

It is worth noting before you choose to use Data Pipeline that, at the time of writing, the service was currently only available in the US East AWS region. As with most AWS services, Amazon typically releases new features and functionality into the US East region first and rolls out the feature to other AWS regions over time. The Amazon EMR CLI covered earlier can be used to create new Job Flows in any of the AWS regions in which you decide to run your Job Flow. Depending on where you run your MapReduce application, this may limit your ability to use AWS Data Pipeline for scheduling your Job Flows. We see real value and potential with this tool even this early in its product life cycle. AWS Data Pipeline can reduce the operational resources needed to maintain

AWS resources by removing much of the additional scripting and applications noted earlier. The potential benefits of this service warrant Data Pipeline's inclusion as a tool to consider in planning your project.

Creating a Pipeline

Like in all AWS services, the first place to start is the Management Console. Choosing Create Pipeline starts the process of creating a new pipeline. Figure 3-6 shows the initial AWS Data Pipeline screen and the example settings used to start the creation of the pipeline in this section.

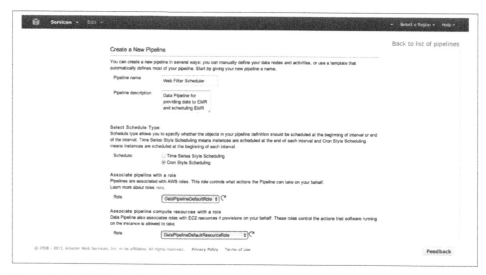

Figure 3-6. AWS Data Pipeline creation settings

Let's review the settings chosen on this initial pipeline setup:

Pipeline name
> This is the name that will appear on the Data Pipeline Management Console and is a user-configured value. Choosing a name that represents the purpose of the pipeline is recommended.

Pipeline description
> This is the description of what the pipeline will be used for, and can be anything that helps describe the pipeline to others who will need to maintain and troubleshoot it.

Schedule

There are two options: Time Series Style Scheduling and Cron Style Scheduling. Time Series Style Scheduling will schedule pipeline items to run after the specified period of time has elapsed. Suppose an item in the pipeline is scheduled for January 1, 2013, at midnight and it should run every hour. With Time Series Style Scheduling, the first time the pipeline item would execute is January 1, 2013, at 1:00 A.M., or after one hour has passed. With Cron Style Scheduling, a data pipeline item will be scheduled at the beginning of a specified period. Using the same scenario, if an item in the pipeline is scheduled for January 1, 2013, at midnight and should run every hour, the first time the pipeline item would execute is January 1, 2013, at midnight. Cron Style Scheduling was chosen in this walkthrough to mimic the scheduling done earlier using cron with the Amazon EMR CLI.

Role

Role controls permissions and security between other AWS services. The security role will be used for any actions taken by pipeline objects. Role settings become important when you are integrating multiple AWS services running at different levels of permission. For this example, we chose the default role setting.

Adding Data Nodes

Choosing Create Pipeline creates an empty data pipeline that is ready to be set up as a workflow similar to what is described in Figure 3-5. We will develop the workflow using data nodes and activities. Data nodes represent the S3 locations the input file is moved to for processing later by Amazon EMR. Data nodes can also represent other Amazon data storage services like DynamoDB or a MySQL database.

The activities represent the actions that will be performed in the pipeline. Copying the input file between S3 locations and processing the data using Amazon EMR will be translated into activities in the pipeline. To start, let's create the input file data node in Figure 3-7.

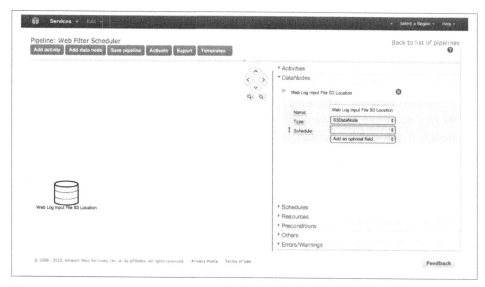

Figure 3-7. Data Pipeline input file data node

In the workflow, in Figure 3-7, we need to specify the input file on S3 and check that the file exists. These are added to the data node via the "Add an optional field" feature. The File Path and Preconditions fields are used for these items. There are numerous other fields that can be added, like Directory Path, which can be useful on data nodes. You can explore and learn more about the Data Pipeline fields and any new additions in the AWS Pipeline Definition Reference (*http://docs.aws.amazon.com/datapipeline/ latest/DeveloperGuide/dp-pipeline-definition-reference.html*). The schedule and preconditions are separate objects that are created in the user interface and can be re-used in other data nodes and activities throughout the pipeline. Figure 3-8 shows the addition of the new fields and the creation of the precondition object.

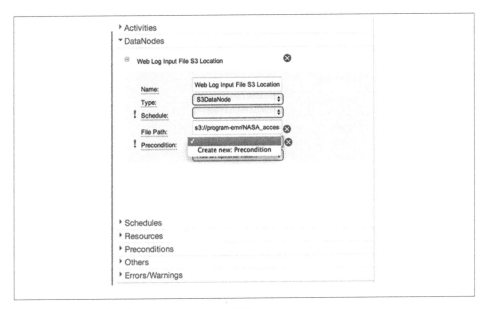

Figure 3-8. Data Pipeline creating precondition

The precondition you created verifies that input file exists before proceeding further. This is a useful check so that the later portions of the workflow will not get invoked and use EC2 or Amazon EMR computing hours unless there is work that is ready to be processed. After creating the new precondition, you can select the precondition object in the "Precondition objects" panel for additional configuration. Use the check type of S3KeyExists to verify the NASA logfile exists and is ready to be used in the rest of the pipeline. Figure 3-9 shows the completed precondition object.

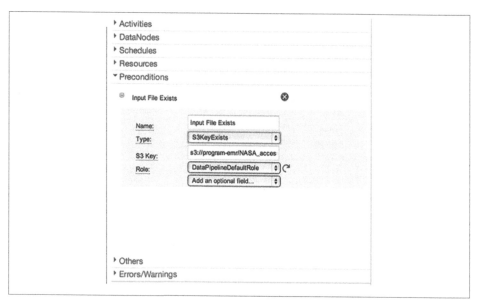

Figure 3-9. Data Pipeline completed precondition object

The schedule object is set up in a similar fashion to the precondition object and will appear in the Schedules panel. The configuration of a schedule is relatively straightforward and does not require the selection of optional fields. Configuration involves setting a start date and an hourly time period (once an hour) to set up a schedule similar to our earlier command-line example. You could add an optional field, End Date, if you needed to limit a pipeline object to a range of dates.

Every data node and activity has a Schedule field and can have separate and different schedules through the execution of the pipeline. It is easy to imagine a different scenario than what we've laid out here. Perhaps your scenario involves input files being copied once an hour and only needing to run the Amazon EMR Job Flow once a day. A requirement like this would necessitate that you create more than one schedule object and set it on activities and data nodes through the pipeline.

The first data node should look similar to Figure 3-10. Throughout the process, you can use the Save Pipeline option to verify there are no missing fields or errors in the pipeline. Any errors or warnings found during saving will appear in the Errors/Warnings panel.

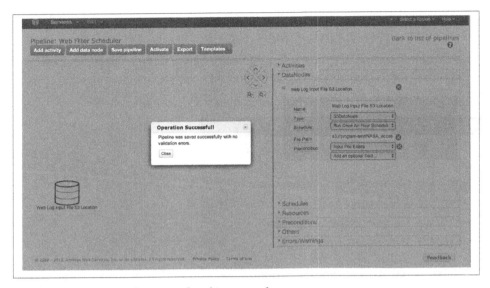

Figure 3-10. Data Pipeline completed input node

In the scheduling scenario, the input file is moved from the location used in earlier examples to a new S3 location for processing. Traditional data processing scenarios move input files to a new location for processing and then archive or delete the processed files. To simulate a similar scenario, let's create an output data node as the output location for an S3 object copy activity. This location will be specified as the input parameter for the Amazon EMR Job Flow. The output data node is set up with the parameters in Table 3-1 to match the section's scheduling scenario.

Table 3-1. Output data node scenario settings

Field	Value
Name	*Web log processing location*
Type	S3DataNode
Schedule	*Schedule created earlier for once an hour*
Directory Path	*s3://program-emr/input*

Now you need to create an activity to perform the actual S3 file copy.

Adding Activities

Activities perform actions on the data nodes or other AWS services. They will need to run on EC2 instances or Amazon EMR clusters, and these services can be set up as resources in the Data Pipeline. From the scenario that is being created in data pipeline, there are two activities that will occur. First, the input file will be copied to the processing location and, upon successful completion of the S3 copy, an Amazon EMR Job Flow will pick up the input data and process it.

You can add these two activities using the Add Activity button. Table 3-2 shows the settings used for the S3 copy activity node and the resources used to run it.

Table 3-2. Activity settings for copying input to new S3 location

Field	Value
Name	`Copy input file to processing location`
Type	CopyActivity
Output	`Web log processing location`
Schedule	`Schedule created earlier for once an hour`
Input	`Web log input file S3 location`
Runs On	`EC2 S3 copy resource`

The S3 copy activity wires together the input and output Data Nodes we set up earlier. Data Pipeline will draw this relationship in the diagram, similar to what you see in Figure 3-11, indicating the direction in which the S3 object will be copied. The result begins to look like a flowchart.

The Runs On field should be configured to the separate resource object that will be used, and you can reuse this throughout the pipeline. The settings for the EC2 resource on the new activity are shown in Table 3-3.

Table 3-3. Resource settings for the EC2 resource

Field	Value
Name	`EC2 S3 copy resource`
Type	Ec2Resource
Role	DataPipelineDefaultRole
Resource Role	DataPipelineDefaultResourceRole
Schedule	`Schedule created earlier for once an hour`
Log Uri	`s3://program-emr`
Terminate After	`30 minutes`
Instance Type	`m1.small`

The Instance Type is set to a minimum setting of *m1.small* due to the limited resources needed to copy data in S3. This can be increased for special situations to improve performance, but in most scenarios a small EC2 instance to move files in S3 should be sufficient.

The Log Uri writes logs to the S3 bucket location specified. This field and the Terminate After fields were suggested additions made by Data Pipeline, but they are not required.

The suggestions appear as warnings when the pipeline is saved. Log Uri aids in troubleshooting if there are issues with the activity, and the Terminate After option allows you to set an upper time limit for the copy operation to complete. This will prevent any runaway EC2 instances due to pipeline failures or S3 issues.

The configuration of the Amazon EMR activity follows a similar pattern, as shown in Table 3-4.

Table 3-4. Activity settings for the Amazon EMR Job Flow

Field	Value
Name	`Amazon EMR web log filter`
Type	EmrActivity
Step	`s3://program-emr/weblog-filter.jar,	com.programemr.weblog_top_ten.We` `bLogDriver,	s3://program-emr/input/NASA_access_log_Jul95,	s3://` `program-emr/run0`
Schedule	`Schedule created earlier for once an hour`
Depends On	`Copy input file to processing location`
Runs On	`Amazon EMR cluster`

The type EmrActivity chosen for this activity tells Data Pipeline that you intend to use Amazon EMR resources. The parameters on an Amazon EMR activity are slightly different from the EC2 resource. The Step option appears as a field, and the settings provided in this example should look similar to the Create Job Flow options set on previous manual runs of Job Flows. Data Pipeline requires that your custom JAR and parameters be combined into a single Step field, with individual parameters separated by commas.

When we laid out the scheduling scenario earlier, we noted that the EMR resources should not be run if the input file did not exist and if the file was not successfully copied to the new S3 processing location. The Depends On option enforces this check and validates that the file has been copied to the processing location by setting the dependency on the successful completion of the S3 copy activity. You can add multiple Depends On fields if your scenario has several dependencies that need to be met prior to an activity running. The Runs On parameter is similar to the earlier activity and is configured to use the Amazon EMR resource with the settings listed in Table 3-5.

Table 3-5. Resource settings for the Amazon EMR resource

Field	Value
Name	`Amazon EMR cluster`
Type	EmrCluster
Schedule	`Schedule created earlier for once an hour`
Core Instance Count	2
Terminate After	`30 minutes`

Field	Value
Core Instance Type	m1.small
Master Instance Type	m1.small
Log Uri	s3://program-emr
Emr Log Uri	s3://program-emr
Terminate After	30 minutes

The Amazon EMR cluster settings look like what was input into the Amazon EMR Management Console in previous Job Flow runs. Core Instance Count, Core Instance Type, and Master Instance Type set the sizing of the Amazon EMR cluster groups. Log Uri, Emr Log Uri, and Terminate After are not required fields, but will again help in troubleshooting by providing log data from the Job Flow and limiting the execution time of the cluster if there is an issue in pipeline execution.

Scheduling Pipelines

Your pipeline now represents the functionality from the initial scheduling scenario and should look similar to Figure 3-11. It is in a pending state right now and will not run until the Activate option is selected. Once activated, the pipeline will appear as scheduled in the AWS Data Pipeline Management Console.

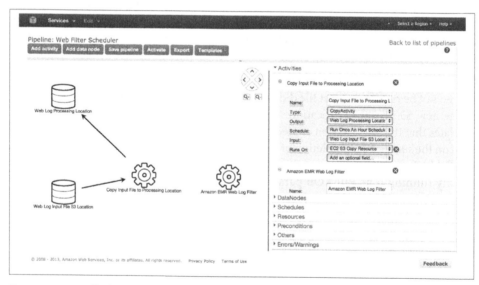

Figure 3-11. Fully built Job Flow scheduling Data Pipeline

Reviewing Pipeline Status

From the AWS Data Pipeline Management Console, selecting View Instance Details next to your pipeline allows you to determine the success and failure of the many different activities and nodes. In scheduling the pipeline, we intentionally removed the input file from S3. Figure 3-12 shows individual pipeline items waiting for the input file dependency to be met.

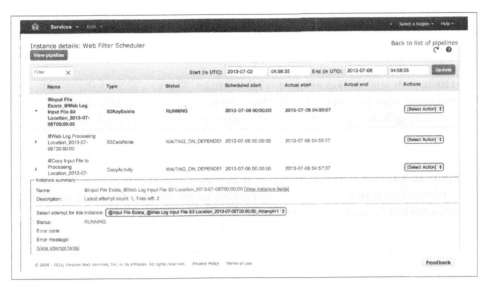

Figure 3-12. Data Pipeline waiting on dependencies

The check for the input file shows as Running, and the details indicate the number of retries AWS Data Pipeline will perform before waiting to try again later. The Data Pipeline Management Console can be used for troubleshooting scenarios like this and to check on successful and waiting pipeline processes.

AWS Pipeline Costs

AWS Data Pipeline is fairly cheap for the functionality it provides. The costs range from free to $2.50 per activity (at the time of the writing of this book). You can find more details on AWS Data Pipeline costs at the AWS Data Pipeline (*http://aws.amazon.com/datapipeline/pricing/*) pricing page. Comparing this cost with the cost of running on the smallest and cheapest EC2 micro Linux instance for the entire month with a total monthly cost of $14.64 (*http://calculator.s3.amazonaws.com/calc5.html*), you can easily see how AWS Data Pipeline can lower operational costs.

Real-World Uses

You have now built a web server processor of the log analysis application described in Chapter 1. Your application can now receive web access log records and review the error requests experienced by users and the frequency of these errors occurring in the log.

The building blocks demonstrated in this chapter have a number of functional uses outside of log analysis. The MapReduce application is performing what is considered both filtering and summarization design patterns by removing unwanted data from the data set and summing up the values of a common key. Other real-world applications of this design technique are:

Data cleansing

Often, data sets contain erroneous information. This can be unrealistic values or too many missing values to be of real use. Performing an initial data-cleansing phase by filtering these values out can lead to better analysis by other applications or other Amazon EMR Job Flows.

Distributed pattern matching

You can look for a specific string or match on a regular expression with a filter pattern. This match can be done in parallel across multiple instances and return matches much quicker than traditional search routines.

CHAPTER 4

Data Analysis with Hive and Pig in Amazon EMR

The examples in previous chapters focused on developing custom JAR Job Flows. This Job Flow type makes heavy use of developing map and reduce routines using the Java programming language. The development cycle of custom JAR Job Flows requires writing map and reduce routines, compiling and packaging the build artifacts, uploading these artifacts to S3, and then creating the Job Flow and retrieving results. This can be a very time-consuming process to explore a data set and build an application. Custom JAR Job Flows can also create barriers for organizations that don't have Java knowledge and experience.

Fortunately, you don't need to be a Java programmer to develop MapReduce applications and use the power of Amazon EMR. Amazon EMR supports several Job Flow application types that we will cover in this chapter, focusing heavily on Pig and Hive application types and how they can be built and tested in Amazon EMR. Pig and Hive are higher-level data processing languages that may be better choices for building Job Flows in organizations that have greater technical expertise using scripting-based languages, or have deep knowledge of SQL for extracting needed data elements.

Hive and Pig will be used in separate walkthroughs in this chapter to rebuild the data filtering and request error counting examples from Chapter 3. The programs will be directly run in an interactive mode on a live Amazon EMR cluster to explore the data set and review the outcomes of each Hive and Pig command.

As you'll see, Hive or Pig Job Flows can be used to build applications that perform many of the same functions that have been covered in this book. They can also be used as tools to perform ad hoc interactive query sessions against large data sets. This chapter will help broaden the toolset that you can use to perform data analytics under Amazon EMR regardless of whether your organization's core strengths are in Java development, scripting languages, SQL, or other programming languages.

Let's start by exploring the Job Flow types available under Amazon EMR.

Amazon Job Flow Technologies

Amazon EMR currently supports four different types of technologies to be added as steps to an EMR cluster. Amazon has worked to tweak each of the cluster types to support interaction with other AWS services and to perform well in the AWS cloud environment. Selection of a particular cluster type is more dependent on the technology needs for your project and the type of application being built. Let's briefly examine the technologies available for steps in an Amazon EMR cluster:

Hive

> Hive is an open source data warehouse package that runs on top of Hadoop in Amazon EMR. Hive Query Language (HQL) is a powerful language that leverages much of the strengths of SQL and also includes a number of powerful extensions for data parsing and extraction. Amazon has modified Hive to work in AWS and to easily integrate with other AWS services. Hive queries are converted into a series of map and reduce processes run across the Amazon EMR cluster by the Hive engine. Hive Job Flows are a good fit for organizations with strong SQL skills. Hive also has a number of extensions to directly support AWS DynamoDB to populate Amazon EMR data directly in and out of DynamoDB.

Custom JAR

> Custom JAR Job Flows utilize core Hadoop libraries that are preloaded into the cluster. A Java application is compiled and uploaded into S3 and is compiled against the Hadoop libraries of the same version used in Amazon EMR. The previous examples in this book exclusively used this job flow technology to demonstrate data manipulation and analysis in Amazon EMR. Custom JAR Job Flows give developers the greatest flexibility in writing MapReduce applications.

Streaming

> Streaming Job Flows allow you to write Amazon EMR Job Flows in Ruby, Perl, Python, PHP, R, Bash, or C++. The nodes of the cluster contain the Apache streaming library (*http://hadoop.apache.org/docs/stable/streaming.html*), and applications can reference functions from this library. When creating a Streaming Job Flow, you can specify separate scripts for the mapper and reducers executed in the Job Flow. Streaming Job Flows are also good for organizations familiar with scripting languages. This Job Flow type can be used to convert an existing extract, transform, and load (ETL) application to run in the cloud with the increased scale of Amazon EMR.

Pig program

> Pig is a data flow engine that sits on top of Hadoop in Amazon EMR, and is preloaded in the cluster nodes. Pig applications are written in a high-level language

called Pig Latin. Pig provides many of the same benefits of Hive applications by allowing applications to be written at a higher level than the MapReduce routines covered earlier. It has been extended with a number of user-defined functions (UDFs) that allow it to work more readily on unstructured data. Pig, like Hive, translates Pig scripts into a series of MapReduce jobs that are distributed and executed across the Amazon EMR cluster. Pig Job Flows are a good fit for organizations with strong SQL skills that would like to extend Pig with UDFs to perform custom actions.

The remainder of this chapter will focus on Pig and Hive applications in Amazon EMR. These job flow technologies most closely resemble the functions and features demonstrated with the Custom JAR Job Flows covered earlier in this book. You can also run Pig and Hive Job Flows inside of Amazon EMR in an interactive mode to develop, test, and troubleshoot applications on a live, running Amazon EMR cluster.

More on Job Flow Types

This book does not cover the details of Streaming Job Flows in great detail. Streaming Job Flows follow a similar development and testing pattern as a standard command-line application, written in Ruby, Perl, Python, PHP, R, Bash, or C++. We recommend reviewing Amazon EMR's sample word splitter (*http://aws.amazon.com/articles/2273*) application or the machine learning examples in Chapter 5 written in Python to learn more about Streaming Job Flows.

What Is Pig?

Pig (*http://pig.apache.org/*) is an Apache open source project that provides a data flow engine that executes a SQL-like language into a series of parallel tasks in Hadoop. Amazon has integrated Pig into Amazon EMR for execution in Pig Job Flows. These additions allow Pig scripts to access S3 and other AWS services, along with inclusion of the Piggybank (*http://aws.amazon.com/code/Elastic-MapReduce/2730*) string and date manipulation UDFs, and support for the MapR version of Hadoop.

Pig performs similar data operations as SQL, but has its own syntax and can be extended with user defined functions. You can join, sort, filter, and group data by using operators and language keywords on data sets.

Utilizing Pig in Amazon EMR

A Pig Job Flow is typically created by choosing Pig Program in Add Step when creating a new cluster, or Job Flow, from the Amazon EMR Management Console. Figure 4-1 shows the initial configuration for creating a Pig Job Flow.

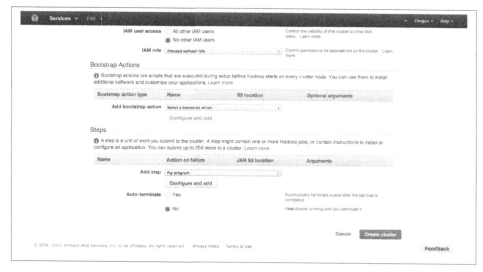

Figure 4-1. Creating a Pig Job Flow

Pig Job Flows can be run as a standard Job Flow where a Pig script is chosen in S3 for execution, and also in an interactive mode. Creating an interactive Pig Session option does not require any steps to be added or configured in Figure 4-1. This is possible because as you recall from our first Job Flow in Figure 2-8 Hive and Pig are installed by default on every new Cluster. The cluster will need to be setup with `Auto-terminate` set to `No` though so the cluster stays running with no steps. In interactive mode, no additional parameters, scripts, or settings are specified under the step `Add and config ure` pop-up. Instead, you can enter Pig Latin commands and parameters directly at the command line on the master node. This starts an interactive Job Flow that waits for a connection to be made, after which you can enter commands into the cluster command line on the master EMR node. The cluster will continue to run until you terminate it using the Amazon EMR Management Console or EMR command-line tool.

The EC2 key pair under `Security and Access` is a required setting on interactive Job Flows—you use it to connect directly to the master node in the Amazon EMR cluster. If no key pair exists or you prefer a new one for your Amazon EMR instances, review Amazon's detailed article (*http://docs.aws.amazon.com/AWSEC2/latest/UserGuide/ how-to-have-aws-create-the-key-pair-for-you.html*) on creating a key pair for an interactive session. You specify the key pair in the `Security and Access` section of the new cluster as shown in Figure 4-2.

Figure 4-2. Specifying an EC2 key pair on New Cluster creation

Connecting to the Master Node

Once the Pig interactive Job Flow has been created, the job appears in a Waiting state in the Management Console, as shown in Figure 4-3. You'll need to establish a session so you can enter Pig commands directly into the EMR cluster. You use the Master Public DNS Name to establish the connection to the master node—this name can be found in the Cluster details page of the console as shown in Figure 4-3.

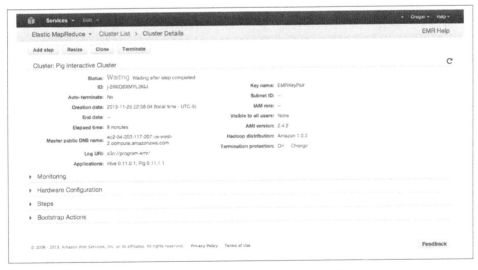

Figure 4-3. Public DNS name for connecting to the master node

With this information, you can now establish a session to the master node using an SSH client and the EC2 key pair. The following example uses a Linux command shell to establish the session. Amazon has an excellent article on establishing a connection to the master node using the EMR command-line utility or other operating systems in its AWS documentation (*http://docs.aws.amazon.com/ElasticMapReduce/latest/Developer Guide/emr-connect-master-node-ssh.html*). After connecting to the node, use the `pig` command to get to an interactive Pig prompt. You should have a session similar to the following:

```
$ ssh -i EMRKeyPair.pem hadoop@ec2-10-10-10-10.compute-1.amazonaws.com
Linux (none) 3.2.30-49.59.amzn1.i686 #1 SMP Wed Oct 3 19:55:00 UTC 2012 i686
--------------------------------------------------------------------

Welcome to Amazon Elastic MapReduce running Hadoop and Debian/Squeeze.

Hadoop is installed in /home/hadoop. Log files are in /mnt/var/log/hadoop.
Check /mnt/var/log/hadoop/steps for diagnosing step failures.

The Hadoop UI can be accessed via the following commands:

  JobTracker    lynx http://localhost:9100/
  NameNode      lynx http://localhost:9101/


--------------------------------------------------------------------
hadoop@ip-10-10-10-10:~$ pig
2013-07-21 19:53:24,898 [main] INFO  org.apache.pig.Main - Apache Pig
version 0.11.1-amzn (rexported) compiled Jun 24 2013, 18:37:44
2013-07-21 19:53:24,899 [main] INFO  org.apache.pig.Main - Logging error
messages to: /home/hadoop/pig_1374436404892.log
2013-07-21 19:53:24,988 [main] INFO  org.apache.pig.impl.util.Utils -
Default bootup file /home/hadoop/.pigbootup not found
2013-07-21 19:53:25,735 [main] INFO  org.apache.pig.backend.hadoop.
executionengine.HExecutionEngine - Connecting to hadoop file system
at: hdfs://10.10.10.10:9000
2013-07-21 19:53:28,851 [main] INFO  org.apache.pig.backend.hadoop.
executionengine.HExecutionEngine - Connecting to map-reduce job tracker
at: 10.10.10.10:9001
grunt>
```

Pig Latin Primer

Now that you've established a connection to the master node, let's explore the Pig Latin statements you'll use in building your Pig Job Flow.

LOAD

The first thing you will want to do in your application is load input data into the application for processing. In Pig Latin, you do this via the LOAD statement. Pig has been extended by Amazon to allow data to be loaded from S3 storage.

As we saw in our previous Job Flows, the data in an application is generally loaded out of S3. To load data into the Pig application, you'll need to specify the full S3 path and bucket name in the load statement. For example, to load *sample-syslog.log* from the bucket *program-emr*, use the following LOAD statement:

```
LOAD 's3://program-emr/sample-syslog.log' USING TextLoader as (line:chararray);
```

The LOAD statement supports a number of load types, including TextLoader, PigStorage, and HBaseStorage. The TextLoader is the focus of upcoming examples, which show its ability to load a data set out of S3. We'll also look at PigStorage and HBaseStorage, which are useful for manipulating the Amazon EMR HDFS storage directly.

Pig Latin uses a concept of *schemas*. Schemas allow you to specify the structure of the data when loading it via the LOAD statement. If your data contained four fields—log date, host, application, and log message—then the schema could be defined as follows on the LOAD statement:

```
LOAD 's3://program-emr/sample-syslog.log' USING TextLoader as
     (logdate:chararray, host:chararray, application:chararray, logmsg:chararray);
```

This can be useful in loading data sets with data structures that map easily to Pig's default schemas. For data sets that don't map to existing schemas, it makes sense to load the data into a single character array for parsing with Amazon's piggybank UDF library (*http://aws.amazon.com/code/Elastic-MapReduce/2730*).

STORE

The STORE statement allows you to write out data. STORE performs the opposite of the LOAD statement and has also been modified to work with S3 and other AWS services. You need the full S3 bucket and location path in order to specify the location of your desired storage output. To write out data to S3, you could use an example like the following to write processed results:

```
STORE user_variable into 's3://program-emr/processed-results';
```

DUMP

DUMP is a useful statement for debugging and troubleshooting scripts while they are being developed in the interactive session. The DUMP statement will send the data held by a variable to the screen.

```
DUMP user_variable;
```

ILLUSTRATE

ILLUSTRATE is similar to the DUMP statement because it is primarily used for debugging and troubleshooting purposes. ILLUSTRATE will dump a single row of the data to the screen instead of the entire contents of a variable. In cases where it may be necessary to verify that an operation is generating the proper format, you may prefer to use this in order to see a single line of a variable instead of millions of rows of potential output. ILLUSTRATE uses the same statement syntax as DUMP:

```
ILLUSTRATE user_variable;
```

FOREACH

FOREACH, as the name implies, performs an action or expression on every record in a data pipeline in Pig. The results of FOREACH are new data elements that can be used later in the interactive session or script. In Pig terminology, this is typically referred to as *projection*. The following example generates, or projects, four new data elements from the RAW_LOG row on which the FOREACH statement operates:

```
FOREACH RAW_LOG generate logdate:chararray, host:chararray,
    application:chararray, logmsg:chararray;
```

FILTER

The FILTER statement allows us to perform much of the data cleansing and removal functions that were done in the custom JAR application. The FILTER statement takes an expression and returns a data set matching the expression. It is similar to using a WHERE clause in SQL, and can contain multiple expressions separated by and or or to chain Boolean matching expressions together. An example of the FILTER statement matching on a regular expression is listed here:

```
FILTER RAW_LOG BY line matches '.*SEVERE.*';
```

The equivalent FILTER statement in SQL would be expressed as follows and highlights the SQL-like nature of Pig Latin:

```
select * from TMP_RAW_LOG where line like '%SEVERE%';
```

To connect the FILTER statement to the concepts you have already learned, we could say that the FILTER statement performs much of the same function as the map phase in our custom JAR. Each row is processed by the FILTER statement and emitted into the variable that holds the results of the filter. From the custom JAR mapper, the FILTER statement is performing the following logic:

```
...
// Filter any web requests that had a 300 HTTP return code or higher
if ( httpCode >= 300 )
{
    // Output the log line as the key and HTTP status as the value
```

```
    output.collect( value, new IntWritable(httpCode) );
}
...
```

GROUP

You can use the GROUP statement to collate data on a projected element or elements of a data set. GROUP can be useful for aggregating data to perform computations on a set of values, including grouping data sets on one to many projected elements. The syntax of the GROUP statement is as follows:

```
GROUP user_variable BY x;
```

The GROUP statement works very similarly to the GROUP clause in SQL. Expressing similar functionality in SQL would yield the following equivalent statement:

```
select * from TMP_USER_VARIABLE GROUP BY X;
```

In the custom JAR application that we built in the previous chapter, the grouping was done for us as part of the key/value pairs that are emitted by the mapper. The grouping is utilized in the reduce phase of the custom JAR to perform calculations on the grouped keys. The following portion of the reduce method utilizes the grouped data to count the number of equivalent HTTP requests that resulted in an HTTP error:

```
...
// Iterate over all of the values (counts of occurrences of the web requests)
int count = 0;

while( values.hasNext() )
{
        // Add the value to our count
    count += values.next().get();
}
...
```

> **More on Pig**
> This book covers Pig briefly to demonstrate one of our earlier build-
> ing blocks that uses Pig Latin. There is a lot more to learn about Pig
> Latin and the many data manipulations and analysis functions in the
> language. To learn more about Pig, see *Programming Pig* by Alan Gates
> (O'Reilly).

Exploring Data with Pig Latin

With a connection established, let's walk through an interactive Pig session to demonstrate the Pig Latin statements in action. This will explore the data set against a live Amazon EMR cluster.

Pig relies on a set of UDFs to perform many of the data manipulation functions and arithmetic operations. In Pig and Amazon EMR, a number of these functions are included in a Java UDF library called *piggybank.jar*. To use these functions, you must register the Amazon library with Pig. You can use the EXTRACT routine in this library to parse the NASA log data into its individual columns using the regular expression from the previous log parsing custom JAR Job Flow. To register Amazon (and any other UDFs), use the `register` statement. The individual UDF statements used should be listed as DEFINEs in interactive sessions and Pig scripts. The following interactive session details the process of registering the library and the UDF:

```
grunt> register file:/home/hadoop/lib/pig/piggybank.jar
grunt> DEFINE EXTRACT org.apache.pig.piggybank.evaluation.string.EXTRACT;
grunt>
```

The interactive Job Flow session that this created takes no parameters to start. To load an input file, use the LOAD statement to bring the web logs into Amazon EMR from S3. The TextLoader takes the S3 location and maps it to the schema defined as a single log line projected by the line name given on the statement as an array of characters (chararray). The RAW_LOGS identifier will hold the data set loaded into Pig.

To verify what has been done so far, we can use the ILLUSTRATE statement to show a single data value held by the RAW_LOGS identifier. Executing the ILLUSTRATE statement causes Pig to create a number of MapReduce jobs in the Amazon EMR cluster, and displays a data row to the screen from the cluster. The following interactive session details the output returned from executing the ILLUSTRATE statement:

```
grunt> RAW_LOGS = LOAD 's3://program-emr/input/NASA_access_log_Jul95'
USING TextLoader as (line:chararray);
grunt> ILLUSTRATE RAW_LOGS;
2013-07-21 20:53:33,561 [main] INFO
org.apache.pig.backend.hadoop.executionengine.
HExecutionEngine - Connecting to hadoop file system at: hdfs://10.10.10.10:9000
2013-07-21 20:53:33,562 [main] INFO
org.apache.pig.backend.hadoop.executionengine.
HExecutionEngine - Connecting to map-reduce job tracker at: 10.10.10.10:9001
2013-07-21 20:53:33,572 [main] INFO
org.apache.pig.backend.hadoop.executionengine.
mapReduceLayer.MRCompiler - File concatenation threshold: 100 optimistic? false
2013-07-21 20:53:33,576 [main] INFO
org.apache.pig.backend.hadoop.executionengine.
mapReduceLayer.MultiQueryOptimizer - MR plan size before optimization: 1
...
...
2013-07-21 20:53:36,380 [main] INFO
org.apache.pig.backend.hadoop.executionengine.
mapReduceLayer.JobControlCompiler - Setting Parallelism to 1
2013-07-21 20:53:36,393 [main] WARN  org.apache.pig.data.SchemaTupleBackend -
SchemaTupleBackend has already been initialized
2013-07-21 20:53:36,396 [main] INFO
```

```
org.apache.pig.backend.hadoop.executionengine.
mapReduceLayer.PigMapOnly$Map - Aliases being processed per job phase
(AliasName[line,offset]): M: RAW_LOGS[2,11] C:  R:
-------------------------------------------------------------------------
| RAW_LOGS| line:chararray
-------------------------------------------------------------------------
|         | slip137-5.pt.uk.ibm.net - - [01/Jul/1995:02:33:07 -0400] "GET /...
-------------------------------------------------------------------------
```

This shows that the logfile is now loaded in the data pipeline for further processing. From the work done on the custom JAR application, we know that the next logical step in the Pig program is to parse the log record into individual data columns. You can use the FOREACH statement with the UDF extract routine to iterate through each log line in RAW_LOGS and split the data into projected named columns.

This should look very familiar because this is the same regular expression from Chapter 3 that you used to split up the data into columns. The data will need to be further typecast to data types that can be used in arithmetic expressions. The FOREACH statement needs to be executed again to convert the HTTP status and bytes columns from character arrays to integers. The ILLUSTRATE statement shows the effect of the FOREACH statement on the data set:

```
grunt> LOGS_BASE = FOREACH RAW_LOGS GENERATE
    FLATTEN(
       EXTRACT(line, '^(\\S+) (\\S+) (\\S+) \\[([\\w:/]+\\s[+\\-]\\d{4})\\]
           "(.+?)" (\\d{3}) (\\S+)')
    )
    as (
      clientAddr:     chararray,
      remoteLogname:  chararray,
      user:           chararray,
      time:           chararray,
      request:        chararray,
      status:         chararray,
      bytes_string:   chararray
    );
grunt> CONV_LOG = FOREACH LOGS_BASE generate clientAddr, remoteLogname, user,
time, request, (int)status, (int)bytes_string;
grunt> ILLUSTRATE CONV_LOG;
-------------------------------------------------------------------------
| CONV_LOG| clientAddr:chararray| remoteLogname:chararray| user:chararray...
-------------------------------------------------------------------------
|         | tty15-08.swipnet.se | -                      | -          ...
-------------------------------------------------------------------------
```

The individual log line has now been expressed as individual fields, and has been converted to Pig data types that allow the log data to be filtered to only the HTTP error entries. You can now use the FILTER statement to restrict the data set down by evaluating the status value on each record in the logfile. The expression—(status >= 300)—maps directly to the logic used in the map routine of the custom JAR to determine which records to emit and which ones to throw away for further processing in the data pipeline. Using the ILLUSTRATE statement, we can assess the logic used in the filter to see the resulting data set:

```
grunt> FILTERED = FILTER CONV_LOG BY status >= 300;
grunt> ILLUSTRATE FILTERED;
-----------------------------------------------------------------------------
| FILTERED| clientAddr:chararray| request:chararray                | status
-----------------------------------------------------------------------------
|         | piweba3y.prodigy.com| GET /images/NASA-logosmall.gif HTTP/1.0| 304
-----------------------------------------------------------------------------
```

Now you can use the DUMP statement to further examine the resulting data set beyond this initial record. At this point, much of the functionality of the mapper built earlier has been covered. So far through the interactive session, the data has been imported into Amazon EMR and filtered down to the records, including records of an HTTP status value of 300 or higher.

In the custom JAR application, you needed to identify a key value so data could be grouped and evaluated further in the reduce phase. The Pig script has not identified any data element as a key in the commands that have been run. The GROUP statement provides a similar key grouping from the earlier application. The request column is the data element to allow the GROUP statement to build a data set for further calculations.

```
grunt> GROUP_REQUEST = GROUP FILTERED BY request;
grunt> ILLUSTRATE GROUP_REQUEST;
-----------------------------------------------------------------------------
| group:chararray | FILTERED:bag{:tuple(clientAddr:chararray,remoteLogname:...
-----------------------------------------------------------------------------
| GET /cgi-bin/imagemap/countdown?320,274 HTTP/1.0 | {(piweba2y.prodigy.com, ...
-----------------------------------------------------------------------------
```

The ILLUSTRATE statement on GROUP_REQUEST shows the results of the data grouping based on HTTP requests. The data now looks very similar to the input to the reduce phase of the earlier custom JAR application.

To compute the total number of error requests for each unique HTTP request string, run the GROUP_REQUEST data through a FOREACH statement to count the number of entries found in the log. The FLATTEN keyword will treat each request in a grouping as a separate line for processing. The incoming data set prior to flattening will be a data *tuple*, or array.

```
Group Key: GET /cgi-bin/imagemap/countdown?320,274 HTTP/1.0,
Tuple:     {(piweba2y.prodigy.com, ..., 98), (ip16-085.phx.primenet.com, ...,
98)}
```

The FLATTEN keyword expresses the array as individual data lines for the COUNT operation to give us a total per request. The result of this operation yields a counting process similar to the reduce routine in the custom JAR application. You can run the ILLUSTRATE or

DUMP statements to validate the end results of the FOREACH statement. Finally, the STORE statement writes the result set out to S3. The storage is handled automatically as part of the custom JAR, but should be explicitly written out with the STORE statement in Pig:

```
grunt> FINAL_DATA = FOREACH GROUP_REQUEST GENERATE
FLATTEN(group) AS request, COUNT($1);
grunt> STORE FINAL_DATA into 's3://program-emr/pig-output';
```

Reviewing the end result set in S3 yields the same results as our custom JAR workflow. The key differences, after we remove the numerous calls to ILLUSTRATE and DUMP, is a small set of nine Pig Latin statements that generate the same output as the earlier custom JAR Job Flow. With the custom JAR program, the process took several develop, build, test, publish, and execute cycles to work out issues in developing the map and reduce routines. With the interactive session, you are able to build and diagnose your application inside of a running Amazon EMR cluster.

Remember to Terminate Interactive Sessions

To clean up from the interactive session, you'll need to choose the Terminate option from the Amazon EMR console. Be aware that, unlike the previous custom JAR Job Flows, Amazon EMR will keep the interactive session running and you will continue to incur Amazon EMR usage charges until the cluster is terminated.

Running Pig Scripts in Amazon EMR

The load and store statements used in the interactive session used literal paths to very specific files stored in S3. To turn the interactive session statements into a Pig script, which can be used in Amazon EMR, you need to modify the literal paths to use the $INPUT and $OUTPUT parameters, which will be passed to the Job Flow when it is created in Amazon EMR. Adding these parameters—and removing the ILLUSTRATE and DUMP statements from the interactive session—yields the following Pig script that can be run in a noninteractive session in Amazon EMR:

```
--
-- setup piggyback functions
--
register file:/home/hadoop/lib/pig/piggybank.jar
DEFINE EXTRACT org.apache.pig.piggybank.evaluation.string.EXTRACT;


--
-- Load input file for processing
--
RAW_LOGS = LOAD '$INPUT' USING TextLoader as (line:chararray);


--
-- Parse and convert log records into individual column values
--
```

```
LOGS_BASE = FOREACH RAW_LOGS GENERATE
    FLATTEN(
        EXTRACT(line, '^(\\S+) (\\S+) (\\S+) \\[([\\w:/]+\\s[+\\-]\\d{4})\\]
        "(.+?)" (\\d{3}) (\\S+)')
    )
    as (
        clientAddr:    chararray,
        remoteLogname: chararray,
        user:          chararray,
        time:          chararray,
        request:       chararray,
        status:        chararray,
        bytes_string:  chararray
    );

CONV_LOG = FOREACH LOGS_BASE generate clientAddr, remoteLogname, user, time,
    request, (int)status, (int)bytes_string;


--
-- Remove log lines that do not contain errors and group data based on HTTP
--    request lines
--
FILTERED = FILTER CONV_LOG BY status >= 300;
GROUP_REQUEST = GROUP FILTERED BY request;


--
-- Count the log lines that are for the same HTTP request and output the
--    results to S3
--
final_data = FOREACH GROUP_REQUEST GENERATE FLATTEN(group) AS request, COUNT($1);
STORE final_data into '$OUTPUT';
```

You can upload this Pig script to an S3 bucket and select it as a parameter in creating a
Pig Program Job Flow. To run the Pig script from the Amazon EMR console, a Pig
Program step is added as a step in the cluster and the Pig script, input, and output files
are specified when configuring the step in cluster creation. Figure 4-4 shows the parameters used in the Pig Program step with the Pig script, input, and output locations
set to the files used from the interactive session. Running this new Job Flow yields the
same results we saw during the interactive session and validates the changes made to
the script to take input and output parameters to the LOAD and STORE statements.

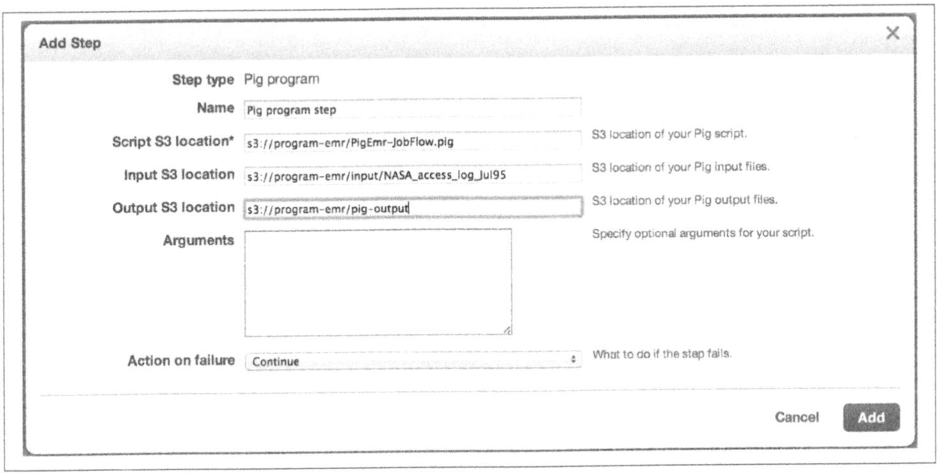

Figure 4-4. Specifying parameters to a Pig script in noninteractive mode

What Is Hive?

Hive is a powerful SQL-like language that allows us to query Amazon EMR. Hive was built to lower the barrier of entry for the large masses of IT professionals who know how to develop in SQL and harness the power of Amazon EMR. The Hive Query Language (HQL) much more closely resembles SQL in feature and function than Pig. The time required for someone who already understands SQL to begin developing in Hive is much shorter than it would be for Pig or Java MapReduce development. Hive is preinstalled on the Amazon EMR nodes in clusters using the Hive Program Job Flow.

Utilizing Hive in Amazon EMR

You'll need to create an interactive session to walk through a number of HQL queries inside the Amazon EMR cluster. You create the interactive Hive Job Flow from the Amazon EMR Management Console. Starting an interactive Hive Session is created in the same manner as the Pig example earlier. A new cluster is created with no steps added and the cluster Auto-terminate option set to No. We can use the same EC2 key pair to access the master node in the Amazon EMR cluster in the Hive session that we used for the earlier Pig session walkthrough.

After connecting to the master node in the cluster, invoke the hive command to begin working with HQL commands directly on the EMR cluster. A connection to an interactive Hive Job Flow will look similar to the following example session:

```
$ ssh -i EMRKeyPair.pem hadoop@ec2-10-10-10-10.compute-1.amazonaws.com
Linux (none) 3.2.30-49.59.amzn1.i686 #1 SMP Wed Oct 3 19:55:00 UTC 2012 i686
------------------------------------------------------------------
```

```
Welcome to Amazon Elastic MapReduce running Hadoop and Debian/Squeeze.

Hadoop is installed in /home/hadoop. Log files are in /mnt/var/log/hadoop.
Check /mnt/var/log/hadoop/steps for diagnosing step failures.

The Hadoop UI can be accessed via the following commands:

  JobTracker    lynx http://localhost:9100/
  NameNode      lynx http://localhost:9101/

-----------------------------------------------------------------------
hadoop@ip-10-10-10-10:~$ hive
Logging initialized using configuration in file:/home/hadoop/.versions/
hive-0.8.1/conf/hive-log4j.properties
Hive history file=/mnt/var/lib/hive_081/tmp/history/hive_job_log_hadoop_
201307220206_218802535.txt
hive>
```

Hive Primer

Now that you've established a session to the master node, you'll use a number of HQL statements to load, parse, filter, group, and output a result set out of Amazon EMR into S3. The statements covered here should look very similar in form and function to SQL. There are some key differences, but looking at the statements needed for a Hive application demonstrates how transferrable SQL knowledge is to Hive development.

SerDe

Hadoop and MapReduce applications that use formal programming languages can work with data with limited structure. The statements and language constructs allow the data to be parsed into a structure the application can work on, deserialize, and then write out later in another format or structure after serialization.

SQL and database systems, however, work with data sets that have a defined structure and set of data types. To allow Hive to have much of the language structure of SQL but still be able to work with the limited structure of data in Hadoop, developers created a number of serializers and deserializers, or SerDes, to allow Hive to input data into a structured format. In the Pig and Java examples throughout the book, we used the individual language constructs and regular expressions to perform the same serialization and deserialization functionality. So, these should not be not new concepts when compared to previous examples.

There are a number of SerDes available in Hive. SerDes are added to an HQL script through add statements at the start of the script. We can use the regular expression used in earlier examples in Hive as well by adding *hive_contrib.jar* as follows:

```
add jar /home/hadoop/hive/lib/hive_contrib.jar;
```

Additional SerDes can be written and included from S3. This is one of the features Amazon has added to support Hive in AWS. Amazon has also provided a SerDe for working with JSON-formatted data. The JSON SerDe can be added to a script from its S3 location in AWS as follows:

```
add jar s3://elasticmapreduce/samples/hive-ads/libs/jsonserde.jar;
```

SerDes define the input and output data formats when you are creating tables to process and query inside of an HQL script. To parse the web logs, your input format needs to specify a regular expression for your log, convert the columns to a set of strings defined by the output format, and number each output column:

```
CREATE TABLE weblog_data(
        host STRING,
        identity STRING,
        user STRING,
        time STRING,
        request STRING,
        status STRING,
        size STRING)
    ROW FORMAT SERDE 'org.apache.hadoop.hive.contrib.serde2.RegexSerDe'
    WITH SERDEPROPERTIES (
        "input.regex" = "^(\\S+) (\\S+) (\\S+) \\[([\\w:/]+
                \\s[+\\-]]\\d{4})\\] \"(.+?)\" (\\d{3}) (\\S+)",
        "output.format.string" = "%1$s %2$s %3$s %4$s %5$s %6$s %7$s"
    )
    LOCATION 's3://program-emr/input';
```

CREATE TABLE

The `CREATE TABLE` statement follows a similar syntax as SQL. The `CREATE TABLE` statement is used for input and output of data from the Hive script with a defined set of data types and structure to the table. The earlier example created a table that maps to the seven columns in our log data and imports the data set into this table from S3.

Amazon extensions to Hive allow access to tables stored in S3 and another AWS service, DynamoDB (*http://aws.amazon.com/dynamodb/*). To create a table handled outside of the HDFS storage in the Amazon EMR cluster, use the `EXTERNAL` keyword when creating the table. This tells Hive that the table exists outside of its storage, and a `LOCATION` is required to tell Hive where the table exists. The following example uses `EXTERNAL` to create a table in S3:

```
CREATE EXTERNAL TABLE MyTable (
        host STRING,
        identity STRING,
        user STRING,
        time STRING,
        request STRING,
        status STRING,
        size STRING)
```

```
ROW FORMAT DELIMITED FIELDS TERMINATED BY ','
LOCATION 's3://program-emr/output';
```

The schema information about what tables exist in Hive is maintained in the master node, and by default is not maintained outside of the Amazon EMR cluster. This means any table that is created in Hive will cease to exist once the Amazon EMR cluster is terminated. You can persist the tables using the `EXTERNAL` keyword to store the data outside of Amazon EMR on S3, Amazon's Redshift Data Warehouse (*http://aws.amazon.com/redshift/*), or Amazon Relational Database Service (RDS) (*http://aws.amazon.com/rds/*).

INSERT

The `INSERT` statement serves the same purpose in Hive as it does in SQL: to place data into storage. Hive on Amazon EMR allows this location to be another Hive table, S3 location, external table, or another Amazon database service like DynamoDB. The `INSERT` statements in Hive take a query as the data source to load data into the storage location. To write the output of a query result to S3, use the following `INSERT` syntax in Hive:

```
INSERT OVERWRITE DIRECTORY 's3://program-emr/hive-output' select * from table;
```

The `OVERWRITE` keyword in the example will replace the data in the destination. The `INTO` keyword could be used in place of `OVERWRITE` to append the data rather than replace it.

More on Hive

This chapter covers only a small portion of what can be accomplished with Hive. To learn more about Hive, see *Programming Hive* by Edward Capriolo, Dean Wampler, and Jason Rutherglen (O'Reilly).

Exploring Data with Hive

You can now put the Hive commands covered earlier to direct use in the interactive Hive session. You'll need to register the SerDe library with Hive so the data can be parsed with the web log regular expression you used in earlier examples. You'll start by adding the contributed SerDe JAR to the session with a simple `add jar` statement and the location of the library on the master node:

```
hive> add jar /home/hadoop/hive/lib/hive_contrib.jar;
Added /home/hadoop/hive/lib/hive_contrib.jar to class path
Added resource: /home/hadoop/hive/lib/hive_contrib.jar
hive>
```

The interactive session has no defined input or outputs. The `CREATE TABLE` statement is used to pull in the web log information from S3. We parse the web log using the regex

SerDe from our library input to separate out each field to map to the table structure. The output format takes each record and maps it to the string data types for each column in the table. The LOCATION specifies the directory where your input files are located.

```
hive> CREATE TABLE weblog_data(
        host STRING,
        identity STRING,
        user STRING,
        time STRING,
        request STRING,
        status STRING,
        size STRING)
      ROW FORMAT SERDE 'org.apache.hadoop.hive.contrib.serde2.RegexSerDe'
      WITH SERDEPROPERTIES (
        "input.regex" = "^(\\S+) (\\S+) (\\S+) \\[([\\w:/]+\\s[+\\-]\\d{4})\\] \
        \"(.+?)\" (\\d{3}) (\\S+)",
        "output.format.string" = "%1$s %2$s %3$s %4$s %5$s %6$s %7$s"
      )
      LOCATION 's3://program-emr/input';
OK
Time taken: 22.122 seconds
hive>
```

Hive does not have the ILLUSTRATE statement like the earlier Pig example. However, you can use standard SQL statements to review the data loaded into the weblog_data table—this was created to confirm the data has been parsed and loaded into the Hive table. Performing a simple count operation shows the full data set has been loaded into Hive:

```
hive> select count(*) from weblog_data;
Total MapReduce jobs = 1
Launching Job 1 out of 1
Number of reduce tasks determined at compile time: 1
...
...
2013-07-22 21:42:12,434 Stage-1 map = 100%,  reduce = 100%, Cumulative
CPU 31.28 sec
2013-07-22 21:42:13,444 Stage-1 map = 100%,  reduce = 100%, Cumulative
CPU 31.28 sec
2013-07-22 21:42:14,463 Stage-1 map = 100%,  reduce = 100%, Cumulative
CPU 31.28 sec
2013-07-22 21:42:15,480 Stage-1 map = 100%,  reduce = 100%, Cumulative
CPU 31.28 sec
MapReduce Total cumulative CPU time: 31 seconds 280 msec
Ended Job = job_201307220201_0001
Counters:
MapReduce Jobs Launched:
Job 0: Map: 1 Reduce: 1   Accumulative CPU: 31.28 sec   HDFS Read: 320
HDFS Write: 8 SUCCESS
Total MapReduce CPU Time Spent: 31 seconds 280 msec
OK
1891715
```

```
Time taken: 149.023 seconds
hive>
```

You can review the individual rows of data using simple select statements to pull back data rows from the Amazon EMR cluster:

```
hive> select * from weblog_data limit 1;
OK
199.72.81.55      -      -  01/Jul/1995:00:00:01 -0400      GET /history/apollo/
HTTP/1.0        200     6245
Time taken: 14.75 seconds
hive>
```

The execution times to run each of these Hive statements may appear shockingly high for such a small data set to anyone who has performed similar queries against a traditional database. The runtimes are high because the Hive command is being parsed and run as a MapReduce job on multiple nodes in the EMR cluster. The execution times are similar to runtimes from the earlier Job Flow applications. A traditional database system that SQL commands are usually run on achieves higher performance compared to Hive due to the structured nature of the data set and system and index optimizations that can take advantage of the structure.

The query entered into the Hive command line is processed and turned into a set of map and reduce jobs. These jobs are executed on each node against a shard of the data set on each node and the end result set is returned. Hadoop does not have the strict data structures and indexing that help a traditional database system perform SQL statements quickly.

Filtering the data set in Hive is as simple as adding a WHERE clause to the HQL query. Using the status column in the table, the expression (status >= 300) will typecast the column and return the matching records. Using the earlier select statement, we can obtain the count of error rows in the log as in the following example interactive session:

```
hive> select count(*) from weblog_data where status >= 300;
...
Total MapReduce CPU Time Spent: 36 seconds 850 msec
OK
190180
Time taken: 113.596 seconds
hive>
```

The map and reduce phases from the custom JAR application can be written into a single HQL statement in Hive. The data filter is performed by the WHERE clause with a check on the status column. You can perform the count and grouping of the data using the group and COUNT(*) from standard SQL data functions and expressions. Utilizing the INSERT statement stores the data to S3 and completes the set of functionality in Hive to replicate the custom JAR Job Flow. The end result set in S3 is the same result set as the earlier Job Flow examples.

```
hive> INSERT OVERWRITE DIRECTORY 's3://program-emr/hive-output' select request,
count(*) from weblog_data where status>=300 group by request;
...
Counters:
15290 Rows loaded to s3://program-emr/hive-output
MapReduce Jobs Launched:
Job 0: Map: 1  Reduce: 1    Accumulative CPU: 36.65 sec    HDFS Read: 320 HDFS
    Write: 0 SUCCESS
Total MapReduce CPU Time Spent: 36 seconds 650 msec
OK
Time taken: 123.133 seconds
hive>
```

To clean up your interactive session, choose the Terminate option from the Amazon EMR console. Be aware that Amazon EMR will keep the interactive session running and you will continue to incur Amazon EMR usage charges until the cluster is terminated.

Running Hive Scripts in Amazon EMR

The Hive CREATE TABLE and INSERT statements need to use the $INPUT and $OUTPUT parameters so the statements used in the interactive Hive session can be used in a Hive script. Modifying these statements and removing the statements used to review the data counts yields the following Hive script, which can be run in a noninteractive session in Amazon EMR:

```
add jar /home/hadoop/hive/lib/hive_contrib.jar;

CREATE TABLE weblog_data(
  host STRING,
  identity STRING,
  user STRING,
  time STRING,
  request STRING,
  status STRING,
  size STRING)
ROW FORMAT SERDE 'org.apache.hadoop.hive.contrib.serde2.RegexSerDe'
WITH SERDEPROPERTIES (
  "input.regex" = "^(\\S+) (\\S+) (\\S+) \\[([\\w:/]+
      \\s[+\\-]\\d{4})\\] \"(.+?)\" (\\d{3}) (\\S+)",
  "output.format.string" = "%1$s %2$s %3$s %4$s %5$s %6$s %7$s"
)
LOCATION '${INPUT}';

INSERT OVERWRITE DIRECTORY '${OUTPUT}' select request,
    count(*) from weblog_data where status>=300 group by request;
```

This Hive script follows the same script execution pattern that has been used by all of the Job Flows. It is uploaded to an S3 bucket and the input and output locations are specified on the step configuration screen in Job Flow creation. The $INPUT and $OUT

PUT variables are replaced with these Management Console values. Running the Job Flow as a Hive script yields the same results and validates the parameter changes made to the Hive statements.

Finding the Top 10 with Hive

Hive can be a powerful tool in lowering the barrier to entry so that many organizations can begin using Amazon EMR to process and analyze data. Hive may also make it easier to build applications that want to focus on data outliers or require data sorting and ordering. Trying to find the "Top 10" is a common scenario that requires data ranking and sorting on a smaller, final data set.

For the custom JAR application to find the Top 10 error records, you'd need to configure the Amazon EMR cluster to have a single reduce routine to collate and sort the results from each of the mappers. You could also do this by building multiple steps, with each step performing a portion of the data manipulation to get to the final list of Top 10.

In Hive, adding the order and limit clause to the HQL statement removes much of the work of figuring out how to configure the map and reduce phases—these are taken care of by the Hive engine. In an interactive session, the Hive engine shows the HQL broken down into multiple jobs to pull back a list of 10 requests that happen most frequently in the web log:

```
hive> select request, count(*) as cnt from weblog_data where status >= 300\
group by request order by cnt DESC limit 10;
...
MapReduce Jobs Launched:
Job 0: Map: 1  Reduce: 1   Accumulative CPU: 36.7 sec   HDFS
Read: 320 HDFS Write: 1031366 SUCCESS
Job 1: Map: 1  Reduce: 1   Accumulative CPU: 5.24 sec   HDFS
Read: 1031843 HDFS Write: 460 SUCCESS
Total MapReduce CPU Time Spent: 41 seconds 940 msec
OK
GET /images/NASA-logosmall.gif HTTP/1.0    21010
GET /images/KSC-logosmall.gif HTTP/1.0    12435
GET /images/MOSAIC-logosmall.gif HTTP/1.0    6628
GET /images/USA-logosmall.gif HTTP/1.0  6577
GET /images/WORLD-logosmall.gif HTTP/1.0      6413
GET /images/ksclogo-medium.gif HTTP/1.0 5837
GET /images/launch-logo.gif HTTP/1.0    4628
GET /shuttle/countdown/liftoff.html HTTP/1.0    3509
GET /shuttle/countdown/ HTTP/1.0    3345
GET /shuttle/countdown/images/cdtclock.gif HTTP/1.0    3251
Time taken: 171.563 seconds
hive>
```

Our Application with Hive and Pig

The Hive and Pig examples in this chapter can be used to replace a number of the building blocks developed in earlier chapters. These approaches do not extend the application, but they allow additional technologies and languages to be brought to bear on analyzing the data in Amazon EMR. You can use the interactive sessions to directly interact with the Amazon EMR cluster and to analyze and examine large data sets using ad hoc queries from the Amazon EMR master node.

CHAPTER 5

Machine Learning Using EMR

So far we have covered various ways you can use EMR and AWS to accomplish some interesting tasks surrounding log data analysis. The next step in building such a system is to begin using machine learning algorithms aimed at predicting things based on your data. In the example for this chapter, we'll use a clustering technique to derive interesting information about accesses to web log data.

A thorough discussion of machine learning is beyond the scope of this book. There are many great resources that will help you understand machine learning. Hilary Mason's An Introduction to Machine Learning with Web Data (*http://shop.oreilly.com/product/ 0636920017493.do*) is a great video course to get started. A more formal treatment of machine learning is available in this Coursera Machine Learning (*https://class.cour sera.org/ml-003/class*) class. It's taught by Stanford professor Andrew Ng and is very accessible to most people—you don't need to be a computer scientist to learn the material.

This chapter will not make you a machine learning expert, but we present a few examples of how to use machine learning algorithms in EMR. Hopefully, this will pique your interest in learning more about this topic.

A Quick Tour of Machine Learning

What is machine learning? Put simply, machine learning is the application of statistical methods to derive meaning and understanding from information. The clustering algorithm we are going to use for this chapter is called *k-Means*. k-Means clustering is used to find a number of clusters, *k*, for a set of data. The exact number of clusters is user-defined—a bit more about this in a moment. The nice thing about k-Means is that you can have unlabeled data and derive meaning from it. This mode of machine learning is called *unsupervised* because no explicit labels or meaning is known ahead of time regarding the data.

As we just noted, k-Means is a *clustering* algorithm. This means it gathers points (your input data) around a predefined number of clusters, *k*. The idea is to help uncover clusters that occur in your data so you can investigate unusual or previously unknown patterns in your data.

The selection of the *k* clusters (or *k*-cluster *centroids*) is somewhat dependent on the data set you want to cluster. It is also part art and part science. You can start out with a small number, run the algorithm, look at the results, increase the number of clusters, rerun the algorithm, look at the results, and so on.

The other aspect of k-Means you need to be aware of is the distance measurement used. Once your data points and *k*-cluster centroids are placed in a space, generally Cartesian, one of several distance metrics is used to calculate the distance of each data point from a nearby centroid. The most common distance metric used is called *Euclidean distance*. Figure 5-1 shows the Euclidean formula for distance.

$$\sqrt{\sum_{i=1}^{n}(q_i - p_i)^2}$$

Figure 5-1. Euclidean formula

There are others distance metrics, which you can discover via one of the two resources listed at the beginning of this chapter.

The basic k-Means algorithm is as follows:

1. Take your input data and normalize it into a matrix of *I* items.
2. The *k* centroids now need to be placed (typically randomly) into a space composed of the *I* items.
3. A preselected distance metric is used to find the items in *I* that are closest to each of the *k* centroids.
4. Recalculate the centroids.

The iterative part of the algorithm is steps 3 and 4, which we keep executing until we reach *convergence*, which means the recalculations no longer produce change or the change is very minimal. At this point we execute the k-Means algorithm. Generally speaking, a concept called *local minima* (*http://en.wikipedia.org/wiki/Maxima_and_minima*) is used to determine when convergence has occurred.

The example that is used in this chapter is based off sample code that Hilary Mason used in her Introduction to Machine Learning with Web Data (*http://shop.oreilly.com/product/0636920017493.do*) video. The code she came up with takes a data file of delicious (*http://www.delicious.com*) links and tags to generate a *co-occurrence* set of tags and URLs. A short snippet from the links file looks like this:

```
http://blog.urfix.com/25-%E2%80%93-sick-linux-commands/,"linux,bash"
http://sentiwordnet.isti.cnr.it/,"data,nlp,semantic"
http://www.pixelbeat.org/cmdline.html,"linux,tutorial,reference"
http://www.campaignmonitor.com/templates/,"email,html"
http://s4.io/,"streammining,dataanalysis"
http://en.wikipedia.org/wiki/Adolphe_Quetelet,"statistics,history"
```

The format basically is *URL,[csv list of tags]*. The co-occurrence is used to find similar things that occur close to each other. In the preceding data set, we are interested in knowing which URLs share the same tags.

 For those of you who want a more formal definition of co-occurrence, you can see its Wikipedia (*http://en.wikipedia.org/wiki/ Co-occurrence*) entry, which states: "Co-occurrence or cooccurrence is a linguistics term that can either mean concurrence/coincidence or, in a more specific sense, the above-chance frequent occurrence of two terms from a text corpus alongside each other in a certain order. Co-occurrence in this linguistic sense can be interpreted as an indicator of semantic proximity or an idiomatic expression."

A nice property of the implementation is that not only are the tags clustered, but so are the URLs. An interesting extension of this k-Means implementation might be to take web server logs and cluster the geographic locations around common resources accessed on the web server(s). This idea has several interesting outcomes, including that it:

- Helps you find what pages are more interesting to different parts of the US or world, thereby allowing you to tailor content appropriately
- Helps you discover possible attacks from known cyberterrorism organizations that operate out of certain geographic locations

It is this idea that we will pursue in the coming section.

Python and EMR

Back in Chapter 3 we showed you how to use the elastic-mapreduce CLI tool. In this chapter, we will rely on this tool again, as opposed to the AWS user interface for running EMR jobs. This has several advantages, including:

- It's easy to use.
- You can keep a number of EMR instances running for a period of time, thereby reducing your overall costs.

- It greatly aids in debugging during the development phase.

Additionally, thus far in the book we have used Java programming examples. In this chapter we'll use the Python programming language to show how you can use EMR to run machine learning algorithms.

 The mrjob (*http://pythonhosted.org/mrjob/*) Python framework allows you to write pure Python MapReduce applications. You can run the code on your local machine (which is great for debugging and testing), on a Hadoop cluster of your own, or on EMR. We are not going to use this tool for this chapter; we are going to use elastic-mapreduce, but just note that it's out there for you to explore and use.

We'll also use the s3cmd command-line tool to upload and retrieve code, data, and output files in S3.

Why Python?

So why use Python? Python has some great capabilities built into it for performing numerical computations. On top of this, the Pycluster (*http://bonsai.hgc.jp/~mdehoon/ software/cluster/software.htm#pycluster*) Python library has some great support for performing k-Means clustering. This framework will be used to run the algorithm. Another nice thing about Python is that, similar to Perl, your development and deployment time are both greatly decreased because you can make code changes and immediately run your application to test or debug it.

 The scikit (*http://scikit-learn.org/stable/*) Python library implements many machine learning algorithms. It has great documentation and a ton of examples.

For the remainder of this section, we will discuss the data input for our application, the mapper code, and then the reducer code. Finally, we put it all together and show how to run the application on EMR.

The Input Data

Recall back in Chapter 2 where we had web log data that looked like this:

```
piweba2y.prodigy.com - - [02/Jul/1995:00:01:28 -0400] "GET ..." 404 -
dd04-014.compuserve.com - - [02/Jul/1995:00:01:28 -0400] "GET ..." 200 7074
j10.ptl5.jaring.my - - [02/Jul/1995:00:01:28 -0400] "GET ..." 304 0
198.104.162.38 - - [02/Jul/1995:00:01:28 -0400] "GET ..." 200 11853
```

```
buckbrgr.inmind.com - - [02/Jul/1995:00:01:29 -0400] "GET ..." 304 0
gilbert.nih.go.jp - - [02/Jul/1995:00:01:29 -0400] "GET ..." 200 1204
```

One of the things we can do is take the co-occurrence Python script and extend it to:

1. Look at the source of the web request.
2. Convert it to a geographic location.
3. Collect the resources accessed from this and other locations.

Note that in the web log data, the first field in the data is the source of the request.

An example data file might look like this:

```
path-to-resource,"csv list of geographic locations"
```

While we don't show it in this chapter, there are open source and commercial geographic databases you can use to accomplish this task.

 MaxMind (*http://www.maxmind.com/en/geolocation_landing*) provides geolocation information for IP addresses. It has both web services and databases you can use. There are costs associated with using such a service, so be sure you understand exactly how you want to use something like this in your application.

The Mapper

Let's take a look at the code for the mapper:

```python
#!/usr/bin/env python
# encoding: utf-8
"""

tag_clustering.py

Created by Hilary Mason on 2011-02-18.
Copyright (c) 2011 Hilary Mason. All rights reserved.
"""

import csv
import sys

import numpy
from Pycluster import *

class TagClustering(object):

    def __init__(self):
        self.load_link_data()

    def load_link_data(self):
```

```
        for line in sys.stdin:
            print line.rstrip()

    if __name__ == '__main__':
        t = TagClustering()
```

This mapper code is really just a shell and is meant for illustrative purposes. It reads the input fed to it on standard in `stdin` and spits it back out to standard out via `stdout`. This `stdout` is then read in by the reducer code—more on the reducer soon.

So what would a real-world mapper do? Here are the bits we're leaving out:

- It would handle parsing of the raw web log data to pull out the source hostname or IP address of the request.

- It would do the geographic lookup for each source and group together resource access by geographic region. This step would be considered a postprocessing step.

- Once done processing all raw log records, it would emit to standard out the resources and geolocations that will feed into the reducer.

Additionally, our example mapper only deals with a single input file. A real mapper is likely going to process multiple, large logfiles. So the input might actually be a directory containing the logfiles to process. The more data you have, especially over a long period of time (one month, two months, etc.), will greatly increase the results of the clustering process.

 If you pass an S3 directory (e.g., *s3n://bucketname/files_to_process/*) to the input option to EMR, it will handle taking all the files in the directory and divvying them up among multiple mapper jobs.

We've put together the following contrived postprocessed data for use in our application. Here is the sample:

```
"/history/apollo/","CA,TX"
"/shuttle/countdown/","AL,MA,FL,SC"
"/shuttle/missions/sts-73/mission-sts-73.html","SC,WA"
"/shuttle/countdown/liftoff.html","SC,NC,OK"
"/shuttle/missions/sts-73/sts-73-patch-small.gif","MS"
"/images/NASA-logosmall.gif","MS,FL"
"/shuttle/countdown/video/livevideo.gif","CO"
"/shuttle/countdown/countdown.html","AL"
"/","GA"
```

Basically what you have is a list of resources along with one or more geographic regions that accessed the resource. We've used US states, but you could also include country codes or other geo-identifiers.

The Reducer

The reducer code is presented next. The first thing you will notice is that it's a little more involved than the mapper code. Areas that need more explanation are called out explicitly.

```python
#!/usr/bin/env python
# encoding: utf-8
"""
tag_clustering.py

Created by Hilary Mason on 2011-02-18.
Copyright (c) 2011 Hilary Mason. All rights reserved.
"""

import csv
import sys

import numpy
from Pycluster import *

class TagClustering(object):

    def __init__(self):
        tag_data = self.load_link_data()
        all_tags = []
        all_urls = []
        for url,tags in tag_data.items():
            all_urls.append(url)
            all_tags.extend(tags)

        all_tags = list(set(all_tags)) # list of all tags in the space

        numerical_data = [] # create vectors for each item
        for url,tags in tag_data.items():
            v = []
            for t in all_tags:
                if t in tags: ❶
                    v.append(1)
                else:
                    v.append(0)
            numerical_data.append(tuple(v))
        data = numpy.array(numerical_data) ❷

        # cluster the items
        # 20 clusters, city block distance, 20 iterations
        labels, error, nfound = kcluster(data, nclusters=6, dist='b',
        npass=20) ❸

        # print out the clusters
        clustered_urls = {}
        clustered_tags = {}
```

```
        i = 0
        for url in all_urls:
            clustered_urls.setdefault(labels[i], []).append(url)
            clustered_tags.setdefault(labels[i], []).extend(tag_data[url])
            i += 1

        tag_list = {}
        for cluster_id,tags in clustered_tags.items(): ❹
            tag_list[cluster_id] = list(set(tags))

        for cluster_id,urls in clustered_urls.items(): ❺
            print tag_list[cluster_id]
            print urls

    def load_link_data(self):
        data = {}

        r = csv.reader(sys.stdin)
        for row in r:
            data[row[0]] = row[1].split(',')

        return data


if __name__ == '__main__':
        t = TagClustering()
```

❶ The point of this code is to create a bit vector to feed into the clustering algorithm.

❷ We must present the clustering algorithm with a vector. This code creates a numpy-formatted array. This representation is much more efficient than using the standard Python built-in array.

❸ Here is where the heavy lifting is done. It makes a call into the Pycluster library function kcluster. Then it performs clustering based on how we configure it. In this example, we ask it to create 6 clusters, use the city-block distance measurement (dist=), and perform 20 passes (npass=). The number of passes tells kcluster how many times to pass through the data until the results converge, (i.e., there is little to no change in the calculations). Recall that the local minima will be used to determine convergence.

❹ This code accumulates all of the clustered tags into a data structure. This acts as a lookup table when we print the clusters.

❺ Using the lookup table of tags, the code prints out the states and the cluster of resources.

The city-block distance measurement is also called the Manhattan distance, taxi cab distance, and others. You can read more about it here (*http://en.wikipedia.org/wiki/Taxicab_geometry*).

As note number 1 in the reducer code points out, a bit vector is used to encode the input data for presentation to the clustering algorithm. If you print the data array, it looks like this:

```
[[0 0 1 1 0 0 0 0 0 0 0 0]
 [0 0 0 0 0 0 1 0 0 0 1 0]
 [1 0 0 0 0 0 0 0 0 0 0 0]
 [0 0 0 0 0 1 0 0 0 0 0 0]
 [0 0 0 0 0 0 1 0 0 0 0 0]
 [0 1 0 0 0 0 0 0 0 0 0 0]
 [0 0 0 0 0 0 0 1 0 1 0 0]
 [0 0 0 0 1 0 0 1 1 0 0 0]
 [0 0 0 0 0 1 0 1 0 0 1 1]]
```

There is one row for each line of input from the data file. Each column represents the set of all geolocations (or tags, from the original implementation). This is *I* from our algorithm description earlier in the chapter. It is done this way because we are not initially starting with numerical data. Because we are clustering on nominal, text data, we must normalize the input data into a format consumable by the distance calculation we chose.

It should be noted that we are not taking into account the frequency of access to a given URL or resource. So if, for example, "/" were accessed a million times, we don't care. Using logistic regression, we could predict the frequency with which a resource might get accessed in the future. The Analytics Made Skeezy (*http://analyticsmadeskeezy.com/2012/10/29/introduction-to-machine-learning-logistic-regression-for-predicting-bad-trips/*) blog has a great example on how to apply logistic regression (and how not to confuse it with linear regression).

As you can imagine, the larger the data set you plan to vectorize, the more memory it will require. This might mean choosing larger instance types with more RAM and CPU power in your EMR cluster.

Putting It All Together

It's now time to upload code and data files to S3 so you can provision the EMR cluster and run your MapReduce job. First, you need to get the Pycluster library installed onto your cluster. The reason you have to do this is because Pycluster is not available to Python on the EMR cluster by default. The way you accomplish this is by creating a script that downloads the tarball, extracts it, and runs the proper Python command to build and install the library. The script looks like this:

```
#!/bin/bash
# pycluster.sh
set -e
wget -S -T 10 -t 5 \
http://bonsai.hgc.jp/~mdehoon/software/cluster/Pycluster-1.52.tar.gz
mkdir -p ./Pycluster-1.52
tar zxvf Pycluster-1.52.tar.gz
cd Pycluster-1.52
sudo python setup.py install ❶
```

❶ Here, the sudo command is used to build and install Pycluster. Without using sudo, the library will be built and installed as the Hadoop user. You want to make sure the library gets installed to the normal location so your script can use it. Usage of the sudo command will not require password input, so it's safe to use in this manner.

You are now ready to upload your input data, mapper code, reducer code, and *pycluster.sh* to S3:

```
$ s3cmd put links2.csv tag_clustering_mapper.py tag_cluster_reducer.py \
    pycluster.sh s3://program-emr/
```

With all the parts in place, you can now turn up the EMR cluster. You will want to create the Job Flow and leave it alive for ease of rerunning the MapReduce application. The following command should hopefully be familiar to you:

```
$ elastic-mapreduce --create --enable-debug --alive \
    --log-uri s3n://program-emr/emr/logs/ \
    --instance-type m1.small \
    --num-instances 1 \
    --name python \
    --bootstrap-action "s3://program-emr/pycluster.sh" ❶
```

❶ This is the bootstrap script you previously uploaded to S3. When AWS provisions an EMR cluster, this script is run. You can run up to 16 actions per elastic-mapreduce command. You can read more on bootstrap actions here (*http://docs.aws.amazon.com/ElasticMapReduce/latest/DeveloperGuide/emr-plan-bootstrap.html*).

Once the EMR cluster is bootstrapped and waiting for requests, you will have the Pycluster library installed and ready for use. This feature of EMR is a great way to get custom libraries and code on the cluster. This is also how you can alter various Hadoop options for the cluster.

You are now ready to run the MapReduce program. Start it with the following command:

```
$ elastic-mapreduce --stream \ ❶
  --mapper s3://program-emr/tag_clustering_mapper.py \ ❷
  --input s3://program-emr/links2.csv \ ❸
  --output s3://program-emr/foo \ ❹
  --reducer s3://program-emr/tag_clustering_reducer.py \ ❺
  -j JOB_ID
```

❶   You are specifying the --stream option to the elastic-mapreduce command. This means you also need to specify the path to the mapper, input data, output location, and reducer code. If you do not specify all four items, the stream command will fail.

❷   This is the location where, upon success or failure, output will be placed.

❸   This is the S3 path to your input data.

❹   EMR will place success or failure status files in the S3 directory you specify with this option.

❺   The reducer code you want EMR to run is passed to this option.

Once your MapReduce job is finished, you will want to make sure you terminate your cluster (recall we started it with the alive option):

```
$ elastic-mapreduce --terminate -j JOB_ID
```

Upon successful completion of the job, the reducer output will be placed in *s3://program-emr/foo/part-00000*. You can download this file for inspection with the following S3 command:

```
$ s3cmd get s3://program-emr/foo/part-00000
```

If your job failed for whatever reason, the files in the S3 directory will look like *part-00001*, *part-00002*, and so on. You can use these to determine why your job failed and go fix the issue.

If you open the *part-00000* file in your favorite editor, you will see the following (note that the output was manually formatted to fit on the page):

```
['SC', 'WA']: ['/shuttle/missions/sts-73/mission-sts-73.html']
['CO', 'AL', 'GA']: ['/shuttle/countdown/video/livevideo.gif', \
    '/shuttle/countdown/countdown.html', '/']
['SC', 'NC', 'OK']: ['/shuttle/countdown/liftoff.html']
['CA', 'TX']: ['/history/apollo/']
['SC', 'FL', 'MA', 'AL']: ['/shuttle/countdown/']
['FL', 'MS']: ['/images/NASA-logosmall.gif', \
    '/shuttle/missions/sts-73/sts-73-patch-small.gif']
```

The output shows clusters around resources and the US states that tended to access them. Some of the clusters are straight out of the data file like that for *SC* and *WA*:

```
['SC', 'WA']: ['/shuttle/missions/sts-73/mission-sts-73.html']
```

But if you look at this line:

```
['FL', 'MS']: ['/images/NASA-logosmall.gif', \
    '/shuttle/missions/sts-73/sts-73-patch-small.gif']
```

It is actually made up of these two data rows from our input file:

```
"/shuttle/missions/sts-73/sts-73-patch-small.gif","MS"
"/images/NASA-logosmall.gif","MS,FL"
```

The results are not perfect. You can see that another *FL* from our input file appears in this output line:

```
['SC', 'FL', 'MA', 'AL']: ['/shuttle/countdown/']
```

Recall that k-Means uses local minima to determine when it has converged. This can cause poor clusters to be formed, which can cause the results to be suboptimal. The bisecting k-Means (*http://minethedata.blogspot.com/2012/08/bisecting-k-means.html*) algorithm is an extension on k-Means that aims to deal with poor cluster creation. The hierarchical clustering (*http://en.wikipedia.org/wiki/Hierarchical_clustering*) is yet another algorithm that can help overcome poor convergence.

What About Java?

The Mahout (*http://mahout.apache.org/*) Java library implements many popular machine learning algorithms with an eye toward running on Hadoop. You can download the source package, build it, and run prepackaged examples. Running Mahout in EMR is also possible, with a bit of work.

What's Next?

This chapter showed the basics of how you can use EMR to run machine learning algorithms. Something worth noting is that not all data sets are amenable to running on Hadoop, especially if splitting up the data set at map time will introduce inconsistencies in the final results. This is also true of machine learning algorithms—not all of them play nicely with the MapReduce paradigm.

For the curious-minded folks, here are three easy steps to becoming a machine learning expert:

- Learn all you can about different machine learning algorithms, including the math behind them.

- Experiment with sample code so you can take theory and turn it into practice.

- Once you are familiar with machine learning, you can start thinking about your particular domain and how you can apply these algorithms to your data.

CHAPTER 6

Planning AWS Projects and Managing Costs

Throughout the earlier chapters, we explored how to use Amazon EMR, S3, and EC2 to analyze data. In this chapter, we'll take a look at the project costs of these components, along with a number of the key factors to consider when building a new project or moving an existing project to AWS. There are many benefits to moving an application into AWS, but they need to be weighed against the real-world dependencies that can be encountered in a project.

Developing a Project Cost Model

Whether a company is building a new application or moving an existing application to AWS, developing a model of the costs that will be incurred can help the business understand if moving to AWS and EMR is the right strategy. It may also highlight which components of the application it makes sense to run in AWS and which components will be run most cost effectively in an existing in-house infrastructure.

In most existing applications, the current infrastructure and software licensing can affect the costs and options available in building and operating an application in AWS. In this section, we'll compare these costs against the similar factors in AWS to help you best determine the solution that meets your project's needs. We'll also help you determine key factors to consider in your application development plan and how to estimate and minimize the operational costs of your project.

Software Licensing

The data analysis building blocks covered in this book made heavy use of AWS services and open source tools. In each of the examples, the charges to run the application were only incurred while the application was running—in other words, the "pay as you go" usage charges set by Amazon. However, in the real world, applications may make heavy use of a number of third-party software applications. Software licensing can be a tricky problem in AWS (and many cloud environments) due to the traditional licensing models that many third-party products are built around.

Traditional software licensing typically utilizes one or many of the licensing models shown in Table 6-1.

Table 6-1. Cloud considerations for traditional software licensing models

Licensing model	Description
CPU	Many software packages license software based on the number of CPUs in the server or virtual machine. To stay in compliance with CPU licensing in the AWS cloud, the EC2 instance or Amazon EMR instances must have the same number or fewer virtual cores. The EC2 instance sizing chart (*http://aws.amazon.com/ec2/instance-types/*) can help you identify the EC2 instance types with the needed number of CPUs. This licensing model can create challenges when the number of CPU licenses forces an application to run on EC2 instances with memory sizes below what may be required to meet performance needs.
Server	In server- or node-locked licensing, the software can only be run on specific servers. Typically, as part of license enforcement, the software will examine hardware attributes like the MAC address, CPU identifiers, and other physical elements of a server. Software with this licensing restriction can be run in the AWS cloud, but will need to be run on a predefined set of instances that matches the licensing parameters. This, like the CPU model, will limit the ability to scale inside AWS with multiple running instances.
License server	With a license server, the software will need to reach out and validate its license against another server either located at the software firm that sells the software or on a standalone server. Software in this licensing model will operate in AWS, but like the other licensing models, it will limit your ability to scale up in the AWS environment. In the worst-case scenario, you may need to run a separate EC2 instance to act as a license server and incur EC2 charges on that license server instance.

None of the traditional software licensing models are terribly AWS-friendly. Such licensing typically requires a large purchase up front rather than the pay-as-you-go model of AWS services. The restrictions also limit the number of running instances and require you to purchase licenses up to the application's expected peak load. These limitations are no worse than the scenario of running the application in a traditional data center, but they negate some of the benefit gains from the pay-as-you-go model and from matching demand with the near-instant elasticity of starting additional instances in AWS.

Open source software is the most cloud-friendly model. The software can be loaded into EMR and EC2 instances without the concern of license regimes that tie software to specific machine instances. Many real-world applications, however, will typically make use of some third-party software for some of the system components. An example could be an in-house web application built using Microsoft Windows and Microsoft SQL Server. How can an application like this be moved to AWS to improve scalability, use EMR for website analytics, and still remain compliant with Microsoft software licensing?

AWS and Cloud Licensing

Many, but not all, applications can utilize the cloud licensing relationships Amazon has developed with third-party independent software vendors like Microsoft, Oracle, MapR, and others. These vendors have worked with Amazon to build AWS services with their products preinstalled and include their licensing in the price of the AWS service being used. With these vendors, software licensing is addressed using either a pay-as-you-go model or by leveraging licenses already purchased (also known as the "bring your own license" model).

With pay-as-you-go licensing, third-party software is licensed and paid for on an hourly basis in the same manner as an EC2 instance or other AWS services. The exact amount being paid to license the software by reviewing the charge information available on the AWS service page (*http://aws.amazon.com/ec2/pricing/*). Returning to the earlier example of licensing a Windows Server with Microsoft SQL Server, a review of the EC2 charge (*http://aws.amazon.com/ec2/pricing/*) for a large Amazon Linux image currently costs $0.24 per hour compared to the same size image with Microsoft Windows and SQL Server with a cost of $0.974 per hour. The additional software licensing costs incurred to have Microsoft Windows and SQL Server preinstalled and running to support our app is $0.734 for a large EC2 instance. These licensing costs can vary based on instance sizing or could be a flat rate. Table 6-2 compares a number of AWS services utilizing third-party software and the AWS open source equivalent to demonstrate the licensing cost differences incurred.

Table 6-2. Open source and third-party licensing costs in AWS

Service	Open source cost	Third-party cost	Difference in cost
EC2	Amazon Linux - Small - $0.06 per hour	Windows Server - Small - $0.091 per hour	52% more ($0.031 per hour)
EC2	Amazon Linux - Large - $0.24 per hour	Windows Server - Large - $0.364 per hour	52% more ($0.124 per hour)
EMR	Amazon EMR - Large - $0.30 per hour	MapR M3 - Large - $0.30 per hour	Same price ($0.00 per hour)
EMR	Amazon EMR - Large - $0.30 per hour	MapR M5 - Large - $0.36 per hour	20% more ($0.06 per hour)
EMR	Amazon EMR - Large - $0.30 per hour	MapR M7 - Large - $0.43 per hour	43% more ($0.13 per hour)

The "bring your own license" model is another option for a select number of third-party products. Both Microsoft and Oracle support this model in AWS for a number of their products. This model is similar to the traditional software licensing model, with some notable exceptions. The software is already preloaded and set up on instance images, and there is no requirement to load software keys. Also, the license is not tied to a specific EC2 or EMR instance. This allows the application to run on reserve, on-demand, or spot instances to save costs on the EC2 usage fees. Most importantly, this allows a business's existing software licensing investment to be migrated to AWS without incurring additional licensing costs.

More on AWS Cloud Licensing

The "pay as you go" prices for the many AWS products that are pre-configured with third-party software can be found on the individual services pricing pages. Third-party software configurations and pricing exist for EC2 (*http://aws.amazon.com/ec2/pricing/*), Amazon EMR with MapR (*http://aws.amazon.com/elasticmapreduce/mapr/*), and Relational Database Service (RDS) (*http://aws.amazon.com/rds/pricing/ Amazon's*).

The "bring your own license" model is a bit more complicated, with a number of vendors having their own set of supported AWS licensing products and cloud licensing conversion. Amazon has information on Microsoft's license mobility program on the site under the topic Microsoft License Mobility Through Software Assurance (*http:// aws.amazon.com/windows/mslicensemobility/*). Information on Oracle licensing can be found under the topic Amazon RDS for Oracle Database (*http://aws.amazon.com/rds/oracle/*) and can be run in either model.

Private Data Center and AWS Cost Comparisons

Now that you understand software licensing and how it impacts the project, let's take a look at the software and other data center components that need to be included in a project's cost projections. For example, consider the cost components of operating a traditional application in a private data center versus running the same application in AWS with similar attributes. In a traditional data center, you need to account for the following cost elements:

- Estimated upfront costs of purchasing hardware, software licensing costs, and allocation of physical space in the data center
- Estimated labor costs to set up and maintain the servers and software
- Estimated data center costs of electricity, heating, cooling, and networking
- Estimated software maintenance and support costs

In the traditional data center, a company makes a capital expenditure to buy equipment for the application. Because this is physical hardware that the company purchases and owns outright, the hardware and software can typically be depreciated over a three-year period. The IRS has a lot of great material on depreciation (*http://www.irs.gov/pub/irs-pdf/p946.pdf*), but by this book's definition, depreciation reduces the cost of the purchased hardware and software over the three years by allowing businesses to take a tax deduction on a portion of the original cost.

When you are running the same application in AWS, a number of the cost elements are similar, but without much of the upfront purchasing costs. In an AWS environment, project cost estimates need to account for the following elements:

- Estimated costs of EC2 and EMR instances over three years
- Estimated labor costs to set up and maintain the EC2 and EMR instances and software
- Estimated software maintenance and support costs

In AWS, there is no need to procure hardware, and in many cases the software costs are hourly licensing charges for preinstalled third-party products. Services like AWS are treated differently from a tax and accounting perspective. Because the business does not own the software and hardware used in AWS in most cases, the business cannot depreciate the cost of AWS services. At first, this may seem like this will increase the cost of running an application in the cloud. However, the business also does not have all the initial upfront costs of the traditional data center with the need to purchase hardware and software before the project can even begin. This money can continue to be put to work for the business until the AWS costs are incurred at a later date.

Cost Calculations on an Example Application

To put many of the licensing and data center costs that have been discussed in perspective, let's take a look at a typical application and compare the cost of purchasing and building out the infrastructure in a traditional data center versus running the same application in AWS.

For a data analysis application, let's assume the application being built is a web application with a Hadoop cluster (which would be an EMR cluster in AWS), used to pull data from the web servers to analyze traffic and log information for the site.

The site experiences the following load and server needs throughout the day:

- During business hours from 9 A.M. until 5 P.M., the application needs eight Windows-based web servers, an Oracle database server, and a four-node Hadoop cluster to process traffic.
- During the evening from 5 P.M. until midnight, the application can be scaled down to four Windows-based web servers, an Oracle database server, and a three-node Hadoop cluster to process traffic.
- During the early morning from midnight until 9 A.M., the application can be scaled down to two Windows-based web servers, an Oracle database server, and a two-node Hadoop cluster to process traffic.

In a traditional data center, servers are typically not scaled down and turned off. With AWS, the number of EC2 instances and EMR nodes can be scaled to match needed capacity. Because costs are only incurred on actual AWS usage, this is where some of the cost savings start to become apparent in AWS—notably from lower AWS (and licensing) charges as resources are scaled up and down throughout the day. In Table 6-3, we've broken out the costs of running this application in a traditional data center and in AWS.

Table 6-3. Comparing application infrastructure costs

	Private data center (initial)	AWS (initial)	Private data center (monthly)	AWS (monthly)
Windows servers	$16,000	$0	$0	$1,218.00
Hadoop servers	$8,000	$0	$0	$648.00
Database servers	$2,000	$0	$0	$421.00
Utilities and building	$0	$0	$1,000	$0
Windows software licenses	$4,800	$0	$0	$0
Oracle software licenses	$1,000	$0	$0	$0
Software support costs	$0	$0	$18	$0
24/7 support	$0	$0	$0	$100
Labor costs	$3,125	$3,125	$9,375	$3,125
Totals	$34,925	$3,125	$10,393	$5,512

In the cost breakout, don't focus on the exact dollar amounts. The costs will vary greatly based on the application being built, and the regional labor and utility costs will depend on the city in which the application is hosted. The straight three-year costs of the project come to $409,073 for the private data center and $201,557 with AWS. This is clearly a significant savings using AWS for the application over three years.

There are two factors left out of this straight-line cost analysis. The costs do not take into account the depreciation deduction for the purchased hardware in the private data center. Also, the accounting concept of the *present value* of money is not included either. In simplest terms, the present value attempts to determine how much money the business could make if it invested the money in an alterative project or alternative solution. The net effect of this calculation is the longer a business can delay a cost or charge to some point in the future, the lower the overall cost of the project. This means that many of the upfront software licensing and hardware costs that are incurred in the private data center are seen as being more expensive to the business because they must be incurred at the very beginning of the project. The AWS usage costs, by comparison, are incurred at a later date over the life of the project. These factors can have a significant effect on how the costs of a project are viewed from an accounting perspective.

A large number of college courses and books are dedicated to calculating present value, depreciation, and financial analysis. Fortunately, present value calculation functions are built into Microsoft Excel and many other tools. To calculate the present value and depreciation in this example, we make an assumption that the business can achieve a 10% annual return on its investments, and depreciation savings on purchased hardware roughly equates to $309.16 per month. Performing this calculation for the traditional data center and AWS arrives at the following cost estimates in Excel:

```
Depreciation savings per month:
( $31,800 Hardware and Software * 35% Corporate Tax Rate ) / 36 Months
= $309.16 per month

Traditional Data Center:
$34,925 - (PV(10%/12, 36, $10,393)) + (PV(10%/12, 36, $309.16)) = $347,435.66

AWS:
$3,125 - (PV(10%/12, 36, $5,512)) = $173,948.69
```

The total cost savings in this example works out to be $173,486.97, even including depreciation. A lot of the internal debates that occur in organizations on comparing AWS costs to private data center costs leave out the labor, building, utility costs, financial analysis, and many of the other factors in our example. IT managers tend to focus on the costs that are readily available and easier to acquire, such as the hardware and software acquisition costs. Leaving these costs out of the analysis makes AWS appear significantly more expensive. Using only the acquisition costs in the example would have AWS becoming more expensive for the database in about six months and for the web servers in about two years. This is why it is critical to do this type of full analysis when comparing AWS to all the major costs in the traditional data center.

This example is still rather simple, but can be useful for developing a quick analysis of a project in comparing infrastructure costs. Other factors that are not included are infrastructure growth to meet future application demand, storage costs, bandwidth, networking gear, and various other factors that go into projects. Amazon has a number of robust online tools that can help you do a more detailed cost analysis. The Amazon Total Cost of Ownership (TCO) (*http://aws.amazon.com/tco-calculator/*) tool can be helpful in this area because it includes many of these additional cost factors.

 Existing Infrastructure and AWS

The example assumes that new hardware and software needs to be purchased for a project. However, many large organizations have already made large investments in their current infrastructure and data center. When AWS services are compared to these already sunk costs in existing software licenses, hardware, and personnel, they will, of course, be a more expensive option for the organization. Justifying the additional costs of AWS to management when infrastructure already exists for a project can be challenging. The cost comparison in these situations does not start to produce real savings for an organization until the existing infrastructure needs to be upgraded or the data center has to be expanded to accommodate new projects.

Optimizing AWS Resources to Reduce Project Costs

Many of the examples in this book have used the default region your account was created in and on-demand pricing for AWS services. But in reality, many of the AWS products do not have one single price. In many cases, the costs vary based on the region and type of service used. Now that we understand the cost comparisons between a traditional data center and AWS, let's review what options are available in AWS to meet application availability, performance, and cost constraints.

Amazon Regions

Amazon AWS has data centers located all around the world. Amazon groups its data centers based on geographic *regions*. Currently, the default region when you create a new account is US West Oregon. Figure 6-1 shows a number of the AWS regions that you can choose when creating new Job Flows, or EC2 instances, or when accessing your S3 stored data.

Figure 6-1. Amazon AWS region selections

Amazon attempts to keep similar AWS offerings and software versions in each of its regions; however, there are differences in each region and you should review the AWS regions and endpoints documentation (*http://docs.aws.amazon.com/general/latest/gr/*

---

rande.html) to make sure the region in which the application runs supports the features and functions it needs. AWS Data Pipeline (*http://aws.amazon.com/datapipeline/*) is one example of an AWS service covered in Chapter 3 that is currently only available in the US East region.

The cost of an AWS service will vary based on the AWS region in which the service is located. Table 6-4 shows the differences in these costs (at the time of writing) of some of the AWS services used in the earlier chapters.

Table 6-4. AWS region cost comparisons

AWS service	US West (Oregon)	US West (N. California)	EU (Ireland)	Asia Pacific (Tokyo)
EC2 Linux large	$0.240 per hour	$0.260 per hour	$0.260 per hour	$0.350 per hour
S3 first 1 TB/month	$0.095 per GB	$0.105 per GB	$0.095 per GB	$0.100 per GB
EMR EC2 large	$0.300 per hour	$0.320 per hour	$0.320 per hour	$0.410 per hour

Looking at these cost differences, you will note there is only a small cost difference between the regions for each of these services. Though the differences look small, the percentage increase can be significant. For example, running the same EC2 instance in Tokyo instead of Oregon will be a 46 percent increase per hour. Let's review the cost of a small data analysis app running in each region using the following AWS services:

- 10 large EC2 node Amazon EMR cluster
- 1 terabyte of S3 storage

Looking at this small example application using the AWS Simple Monthly Calculator (*http://calculator.s3.amazonaws.com/calc5.html*), you can see that the small difference in the costs in each region for an app can cause the real costs to vary by thousands of dollars per year, simply depending on the region in which the application is run. Table 6-5 shows how the costs can add up simply by changing AWS regions.

Table 6-5. Example app monthly costs per region

US West (Oregon)	US West (N. California)	EU (Ireland)	Asia Pacific (Tokyo)
$2,519.59 per month	$2,691.57 per month	$2,680.63 per month	$3,410.77 per month

Of course, cost is only one factor to consider in picking a region for the application. Performance and availability could be more important factors that may outweigh some of the cost differences. Also, where your data is actually located (aka *data locality*), the type of data you are processing, and what you plan to do with your results are other key factors to include in selecting a region. The time it takes to transfer your data to the US, or country-specific rules like the EU Data Protection Directive (*http://ec.europa.eu/justice/data-protection/index_en.htm*), may make it prohibitive for you to transfer your data to the cheapest AWS region. All of these factors need to be considered before you just pick the lowest cost region.

Amazon Availability Zones

Amazon also has several availability *zones* within each region. Zones are separate data centers in the same region. Amazon regions are completely isolated from one another, and the failure in one region does not affect another—this is not necessarily the case for zones. These items are important in how you design your application for redundancy and failure. For mission-critical applications, you should run your application in multiple regions and multiple zones in each region. This will allow the application to continue to run if a region or a zone experiences issues. This is a rare, but not completely unheard of, event. The most recent high-profile outage of an AWS data center was the infamous Christmas Eve 2012 outage (*http://www.forbes.com/sites/kellyclay/2012/12/24/amazon-aws-takes-down-netflix-on-christmas-eve/*) that affected Netflix servers in the US East (N. Virginia) region.

Maintaining availability of your app and continued data processing is important. Zones and regions may seem less important because you aren't running the data centers. However, these become useful concepts to be aware of because running an application in multiple regions or availability zones can increase the overall AWS charges incurred by the application. For example, if an application was already using AWS services for a number of other projects in one region in it may make sense to continue to use this same region for other AWS projects. Amazon currently charges $0.02 per gigabyte for US West (Oregon) to move your S3 data to another Amazon region. Other services, like Amazon's Relational Database Service (RDS), have higher charges for multi-availability zone deployments.

EC2 and EMR Costs with On Demand, Reserve, and Spot Instances

Many of the earlier examples focused on EC2 and EMR instance sizes. Amazon also has a number of pricing models depending on a project's instance availability needs and whether an organization is willing to pay some upfront costs to lower hourly usage costs. Amazon offers the following pricing models for EC2 and EMR instances:

Pay as you go: on-demand
> With on-demand instances, Amazon allows you to use EC2 and EMR instances in its data center without any upfront costs. Costs are only incurred as resources are used. If the application being built has a limited lifespan, or a proof of concept needs to be developed to demonstrate the value of a potential project, on-demand instances may be the best choice.

Reserve instances
> With reserve instances, an upfront cost is paid for instances that will be used on a project. This is very similar to the traditional data center model, but can be a good choice to match an organization's internal annual budgeting and purchasing processes. A one-year or three-year agreement with Amazon can reserve a number of instances. Purchasing reserve instances lowers the hourly usage rate in some cases

to as low as 30% of what would be paid for on-demand instances. Reserve instances can greatly lower costs if the application is long-term and the EC2 and EMR capacity needs are well known over a number of months or years.

Spot instances

Spot instances allow an organization to bid on the price for the spare EC2 or EMR compute capacity that exists at the time within AWS. Using spot instances can significantly lower the cost of an application's operation if the application can gracefully deal with instance failure and has flexibility in the amount of time it takes to complete a Job Flow or the operations inside an EC2 instance. Spot instances become available once the going rate is equal to or less than the target price. However, once the target price goes above a bid price, the spot instances will be terminated. Task instances from the EMR examples are perfect candidates for spot instances in Amazon EMR Job Flows because they do not hold persistent data and can be terminated without causing a Job Flow to fail.

Reserve Instances

If an application will run for an extended period of time every month, using reserved instances is probably the most cost-effective option for an application. The hourly charges are lower, and reserve instances are not subject to early termination like spot instances. Reserve instances are purchased directly through the EC2 dashboard (see Figure 6-2).

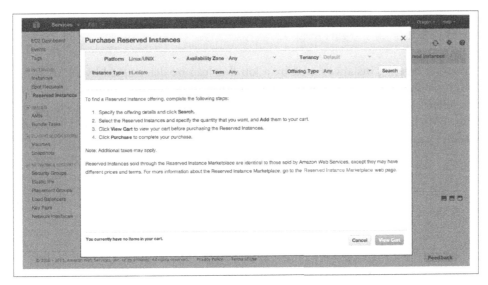

Figure 6-2. Purchasing AWS reserve instances

There are a number of key items to be aware of when you are purchasing reserve instances. Figure 6-2 shows purchasing reserve instances in a specific zone in a specific region. This is important because when a Job Flow is created, it needs to use instances from the same availability zone in order to use the purchased reserve instances. If a different availability zone is chosen or you allow Amazon to choose one for you, the Job Flow will be charged the on-demand rate for any EC2 instances used in EMR.

Currently the only ways of specifying the availability zone when launching a new cluster, or Job Flow, is by specifying the availability zone in the Hardware Configuration when creating a new cluster, using the Elastic MapReduce command-line tool (*http://aws.amazon.com/developertools/2264*) or the AWS SDK (*http://aws.amazon.com/sdkforjava/*). Example 6-1 shows creating a Job Flow using the command line. The availability-zone option specifies the zone in which the job is created so the reserved instances can be used.

Example 6-1. Specifying an availability zone on a Job Flow

```
hostname$ elastic-mapreduce --create --name "Program EMR Job Flow Reserve"
--num-instances 3
--availability-zone us-west-2a ❶
--jar s3n://program-emr/log-analysis.jar
--main-class com.programemr.LogAnalysisDriver
--arg "s3n://program-emr/sample-syslog.log"
--arg "s3n://program-emr/run0"
Created job flow j-2ZBQDXX8BQQW2
```

❶ The availability-zone argument lets you specify the exact zone where you want to create a Job Flow. This can allow you to use a purchased reserved instance in EMR.

The exact types of instances used by a job flow can be determined by running the command-line utility with the describe command-line option. Information is also available by reviewing the Hardware Configuration section in the Cluster Details page in the EMR Console. Figure 6-3 shows information on the cluster groups, bid price, and instance counts used.

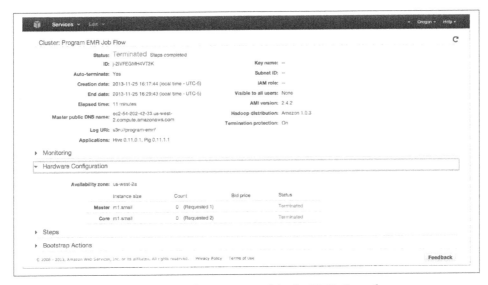

Figure 6-3. Reviewing instance information used in the EMR Console

Spot Instances

Spot instances can make sense for task instances because they do not hold persistent data like the core and master nodes of the EMR cluster. The termination of a task node will not cause the entire Job Flow to terminate.

Technically, you can select spot instances for any of the nodes in the cluster, and use them via the EMR Management Console, CLI, or the AWS SDK. In bidding for spot instances, you can check the current price by checking the AWS spot instance page (*http://aws.amazon.com/ec2/spot-instances/*) for your region. Figure 6-4 shows using spot instances for the task nodes and setting a bid price of $0.01.

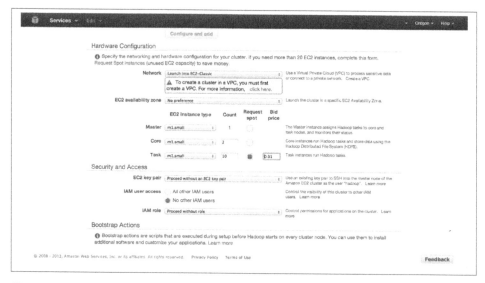

Figure 6-4. Using spot instances when creating a Job Flow

Additional spot instances—or really any instance type—can be added to a Job Flow that is currently running. This may be useful if an application is getting behind and additional capacity is needed to reduce a backlog of work. This functionality is available using the `Resize` button on the Cluster Details page of a running Job Flow, the command-line tool, or the AWS API. Here is an example of adding five spot task instances to a running Job Flow:

```
./elastic-mapreduce --jobflow JobFlowId \ --add-instance-group task --
instance-type m1.small \ --instance-count 5 --bid-price 0.01
```

Reducing AWS Project Costs

There are a number of key areas you can focus on to reduce the execution costs of an AWS project using EC2 and EMR. Keeping the following items in mind during development and operation can reduce the monthly AWS charges incurred by an application.

EMR and EC2 usage billed by the hour

One of the quirks in how AWS charges for services is that EC2 and EMR usage is charged on an hourly basis. So if application fires up a test using a 10-instance EMR cluster that immediately fails and has an actual runtime of only one minute, you will still be charged for 10 hours of usage. This is one hour for each instance that ran for one minute. If the application is started again 10 minutes later, the remaining time left in the hour cannot be reclaimed by the newly running instances and new charges are incurred. To reduce this effect, you can do the following on your project:

- Use the minimum cluster size when developing an application in AWS. The application can be scaled up once it is ready to launch for production usage or load testing.

- Amazon EMR allows Job Flow usage to be monitored through its monitoring tool CloudFront. There is CloudFront Monitoring for Job Flows in the `Monitoring` section of the Cluster Details page, as shown in Figure 6-5. You can review Job Flow usage and verify how much of your Job Flow activity is processing data instead of waiting for data to arrive. This allows the application to be monitored over time so resources can be increased or decreased as load varies over the life of the application.

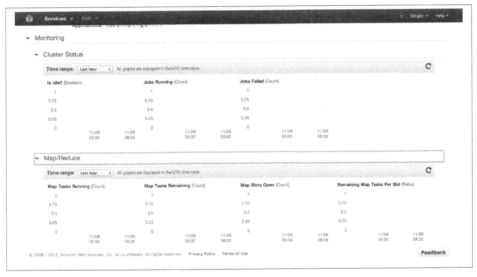

Figure 6-5. CloudFront monitoring of a Job Flow

 Setting the Amazon EMR cluster size to a node level equal to or less than the expected volume can lead to significant cost savings. An Amazon EMR cluster can be resized after it has been started, but you will typically only want to increase the cluster size. Reducing the number of data nodes in an Amazon EMR cluster can lead to Job Flow failure or data loss. For more information on resizing an Amazon EMR cluster, review Amazon's article (*http://docs.aws.amazon.com/Elastic MapReduce/latest/DeveloperGuide/emr-manage-resize.html*) on resizing a running cluster.

Cost efficiencies with reserved and spot instances

Earlier in the chapter, we discussed the different instance purchasing options and how these instance types could be used by the application. To help users better understand the costs with different execution scenarios, Amazon provides a general guide (*http://aws.amazon.com/ec2/reserved-instances/*) to help you decide when purchasing reserved instances would be the right choice to lower the operational costs of running AWS services.

Using the small data analysis application discussed earlier in the chapter, let's review a number of scenarios of running the application in each region using the following AWS services for 50% of the month.

- 10 large EC2 node Amazon EMR cluster
- 1 terabyte of S3 storage

In the case of on-demand instances we can use, the AWS Simple Monthly Calculator (*http://calculator.s3.amazonaws.com/calc5.html*) to calculate the monthly costs incurred. There are no upfront costs for on-demand instances, only monthly costs for usage of the instances.

If you are willing to pay an upfront cost to get reserved EC2 capacity, you can get a lower hourly charge per EC2 instance. This lowers the monthly utilization costs for instances. Using reserved instances and assuming we will fall under Amazon's heavy utilization category, you can see the costs start to come down, even with only 50% monthly usage, in Table 6-6.

However, we can gain the greatest cost savings by combining the use of reserved instances and spot instances. If your application has fluctuating loads or there is flexibility in the time to complete the work in the Job Flows, a portion of the capacity could be allocated as spot instances. Looking at this scenario using current spot prices, we can see that the hourly cost savings approach the cost of reserved instances without the upfront costs. Of course, the benefits of this structure are dependent on the availability and prices of spot instances. Table 6-6 shows the cost comparisons of the same application utilizing each of these cost options.

Table 6-6. AWS on-demand, reserved, and spot instance cost scenarios

AWS on-demand service	Costs	AWS reserved service	Costs	AWS reserved and spot service	Costs
10 EC2 large upfront cost	$0	10 EC2 large upfront cost	$10,280.00	5 EC2 large upfront cost	$5,140.00
10 EC2 Linux large	$878.41	10 EC2 reserved Linux large	$336.72	5 EC2 reserved Linux large	$168.36
0 EC2 Linux spot large	$0	0 EC2 Linux spot large	$0	5 EC2 Linux spot large	$141.12
S3 1 TB	$95.00	S3 1 TB	$95.00	S3 1 TB	$95.00
Total for 3 years	$35,042.76	Total for 3 years	$25,821.92	Total for 3 years	$19,701.28

AWS on-demand service	Costs	AWS reserved service	Costs	AWS reserved and spot service	Costs
Total per month	$973.41	Total per month	$431.72	Total per month	$404.48
Total for 3 years	$35,042.76	Total for 3 years	$25,821.92	Total for 3 years	$19,701.28

 In general, if an application is up and running and consuming EC2 or EMR hours for more than 40% of the month, it makes sense to start purchasing reserved instances to save on monthly charges. Amazon lists the break-even points between on-demand instances and the various reserved utilization levels on the AWS EC2 website (*http:// aws.amazon.com/ec2/reserved-instances/*).

Project storage costs

Data analysis projects tend to consume vast amounts of storage. Amazon provides a number of storage options to retain data and classifies the storage options as standard, reduced redundancy, and Glacier storage. Let's look at each of these and review the benefits and costs of each option.

Standard storage

This is the default storage on anything stored in S3. Standard storage items are replicated within the same facility and across several availability zones, so the data has a very low likelihood of being lost. This type of storage is great if this is a primary resource for the data that is not stored durably somewhere else. Standard storage is also a good option if data lives only in the cloud or the cost and time of reloading the data into S3 is too high to sustain a loss. Standard storage is the most expensive S3 storage option, however.

Reduced redundancy storage

Data can also be stored with less redundancy in S3. Standard storage makes three copies of a data element in a region, whereas reduced redundancy storage makes only two copies of the data. This is still fairly robust durability. Reduced redundancy can be set on any object uploaded to S3. This type of storage may be good if the data is stored somewhere else in a durable manner or if the data has a limited lifespan. Reduced redundancy storage is roughly 25% cheaper than standard storage.

Glacier storage

Glacier is Amazon's data archival service. Data stored in Glacier may take several hours to retrieve and is best for data that is rarely accessed. This type of storage is best for data that has already been processed, but may need to be retained for compliance purposes or to generate reports at a later point in time. Glacier is Amazon's lowest cost storage option at only $0.01 per gigabyte.

Data life cycles

In many projects, you process your data and then need to retain that data for a number of years, often for compliance or reporting reasons. Keeping this data around where it is immediately available and stored on standard storage can become very expensive. In S3, you can set up a data life cycle policy on each of your S3 buckets. With a life cycle rule, you can have Amazon automatically delete or move your data to Glacier after a predefined time period. Figure 6-6 shows the configuration setting for a retention period of 60 days. A rule can be created on any bucket in S3 to move data to Glacier after a configurable period of time.

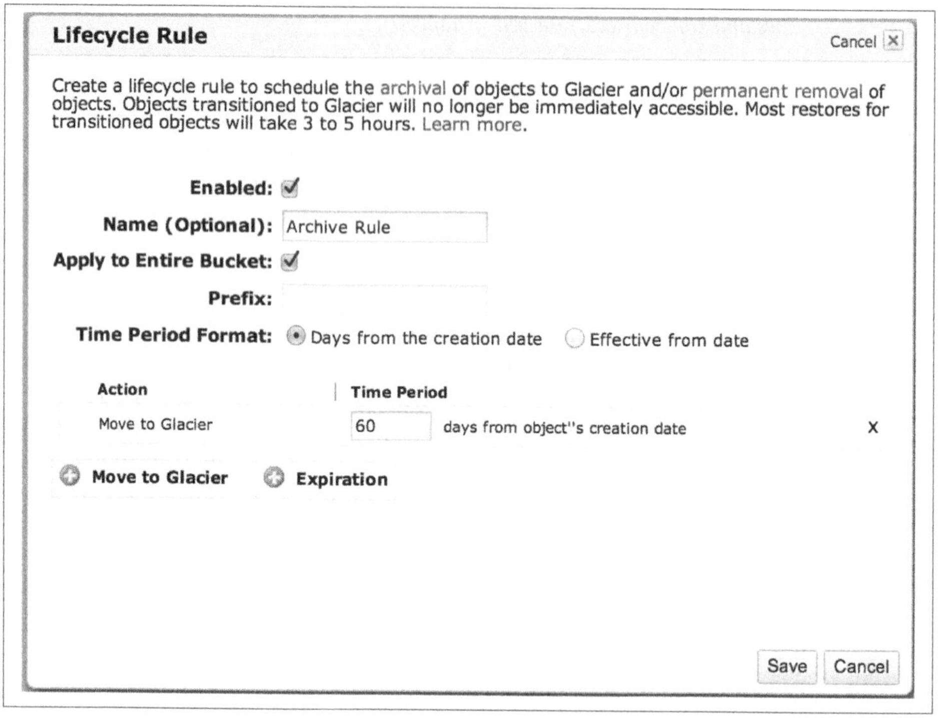

Figure 6-6. Defining an S3 life cycle rule

Let's look at an example of how this will save on project costs.

Consider an organization with a one-year data retention policy that receives one terabyte of data every month, but only needs to generate a report at the end of each month. The organization keeps two months of data on live S3 storage in case the previous month's report needs to be rerun. At the end of this year, 12 terabytes of data are stored at Amazon. Table 6-7 shows the cost comparisons of different storage policies and how you can achieve cost savings using a data life cycle policy while still allowing the most recent data to be immediately retrievable.

Table 6-7. Data storage cost comparisons

Storage strategy	Annual cost
1TB per month using S3 standard storage only	$6,420
1TB per month using S3 reduced redundancy storage only	$5,136
1TB per month using Glacier storage only	$780
1TB per month using S3 standard storage with Glacier 60-day retention	$2,735

Amazon Tools for Estimating Your Project Costs

This chapter covered a number of key factors in evaluating a project in the traditional data center and using AWS services. The examples used in this chapter may vary greatly from the application for your organization. The following Amazon tools were used to demonstrate many of the scenarios in this chapter and will be useful in estimating costs for your project:

Amazon's Total Cost of Ownership calculator (http://aws.amazon.com/tco-calculator/)
> This is useful in comparing AWS costs to traditional data center costs for an application.

AWS Simple Monthly Calculator (http://calculator.s3.amazonaws.com/calc5.html)
> This helps develop monthly cost estimates for AWS services, and scenarios can be saved and sent to others in the organization.

Try these tools out on your project and see what solutions will work best for your organization.

Amazon Web Services Resources and Tools

Throughout the book, we provided a number of the AWS links and demonstrated the tools. This appendix serves as a snapshot of resources that are useful for planning and building applications utilizing Amazon EMR and various other supporting services and information.

Amazon AWS Online Resources

The examples and information represented costs and services available at the time of writing this book. Amazon regularly adds services, new service options, and competitive pricing. We strongly recommend reviewing the latest information on AWS before starting your project.

The following links and information on Amazon's AWS site should be helpful in using and understanding the services in this book.

Amazon Web Services (AWS) home page (http://aws.amazon.com/)
This is a starting point for learning about Amazon Web Services and signing up for service.

Amazon Elastic MapReduce (EMR) (http://aws.amazon.com/elasticmapreduce/)
This is the service home page for Amazon Elastic MapReduce. The site provides a detailed description of Amazon Elastic MapReduce, third-party software installation options, and detailed pricing and configuration information.

Amazon Elastic Compute Cloud (EC2) (http://aws.amazon.com/ec2/)
This is the service home page for Amazon Elastic Compute Cloud. The site provides a detailed description of Amazon EC2 and detailed pricing information. Amazon EC2 is used for a number of the source machines and to run tasks separate from Amazon EMR throughout the book.

Amazon Simple Storage Service (http://aws.amazon.com/s3/)

This is the service home page for Amazon Simple Storage Service (S3). The site provides a detailed description of Amazon S3 and pricing information. Amazon S3 is used to store input and output data for Amazon EMR data analysis. Many of the scripts and applications used for data analysis are stored in S3, and their S3 location is specified in configuring Amazon EMR Job Flows.

Amazon Glacier (http://aws.amazon.com/glacier/)

This is the service home page for Amazon Glacier. Amazon Glacier is a low-cost, long-term storage solution for data in the book that may be needed in the future, but is not currently being processed by EMR or reviewed by system users. Amazon Glacier can be used for cost savings compared to online S3 storage.

AWS Data Pipeline (http://aws.amazon.com/datapipeline/)

This is the service home page for AWS Data Pipeline. Data Pipeline is used to automate EMR processing and reduce the administrative burden of maintaining an EMR application in AWS.

Amazon AWS Cost Estimation Tools

When one transitions from internal systems to cloud-based solutions like AWS, the discussion almost always comes down to considerations around cost. In Chapter 6, we covered numerous real-world scenarios and estimation techniques to review project costs. In running through the scenarios, we used the following online cost estimation tools to review and compare costs in the scenarios.

Amazon Web Services Simple Monthly Calculator (http://calculator.s3.amazo naws.com/calc5.html)

This online calculator allows you to input the resources you expect to use in AWS and determine the monthly cost of those services. The tool also allows you to "Save and Share" your calculations, and produces a URL that can be given to others on the project team or stakeholders for review.

Amazon Web Services Economics Center (http://aws.amazon.com/economics/)

The Economics Center helps you compare the costs of running an application in a traditional data center and running the same application in AWS. This tool can be useful in determining cost savings and comparing available resources inside an organization.

AWS Best Practices and Architecture

Amazon provides a number of critical documents that help organizations start building their applications using best practices. Also, for organizations that use third-party components like Microsoft Windows, Oracle, Red Hat Linux, and others, Amazon provides a number of already configured EC2 instances and information on how to build your own Amazon Machine Images (AMI). The following links at AWS are useful for projects that need this information:

Amazon Architecture Center (http://aws.amazon.com/architecture/)
This AWS site helps developers review software reference architectures that were designed to make best use of AWS services. The site can be useful in building a new application or transitioning an existing application over to AWS. The information will help the development team build applications in AWS that minimize downtime and optimize scalability and performance.

Amazon Security Center (https://aws.amazon.com/security/)
Security is one of the top reasons many organizations have been hesitant to move their critical systems to cloud service providers like AWS. Amazon provides a great deal of information on the security of AWS and its AWS data centers on this site. Information on how AWS meets the compliance regulations for a number of industry compliance regimes like PCI, HIPAA, and others is also published on this site.

Amazon EC2 Instances (http://aws.amazon.com/ec2/instance-types/)
This site demystifies the Amazon EC2 instance sizes of small, medium, large, extra large, and so on, and maps these sizes to their physical equivalents of CPU, memory, and disk space allocations.

Create Your Own AMI (http://docs.aws.amazon.com/AWSEC2/latest/UserGuide/creating-an-ami.html)
Amazon AWS has many of the common software configurations that many organizations use for applications. However, you may want to build an Amazon Machine Image of special or in-house software so you can instantly start a preconfigured image with your software. This guide provides details on how to build a custom image to run inside EC2 or EMR.

Amazon EMR Distributions

As a developer in Amazon EMR, you must understand what features and APIs are available. Fortunately, Amazon has extensive documentation of all of its AWS services including developer documentation (*http://aws.amazon.com/documentation/elastic mapreduce/*) of EMR.

Amazon regularly updates the version of Hadoop and applies patches to integrate Hadoop with AWS infrastructure and services. Table A-1 lists the versions of Hadoop that are supported in Amazon EMR as of the writing of this book.

Table A-1. Amazon-supported Hadoop versions

Hadoop version	Configuration parameters
1.0.3	--hadoop-version 1.0.3 --ami-version 2.3
0.20.205	--hadoop-version 0.20.205 --ami-version 2.0
0.20	--hadoop-version 0.20 --ami-version 1.0
0.18	--hadoop-version 0.18 --ami-version 1.0

To find out the latest supported versions of Hadoop for EMR, visit the Supported Hadoop Versions (*http://docs.aws.amazon.com/ElasticMapReduce/latest/Developer Guide/emr-plan-hadoop-version.html*) section of the EMR Developer Guide.

Cloud Computing, Amazon Web Services, and Their Impacts

Though cloud computing was originally conceived in the 1960s by pioneering thinkers (*http://www.forbes.com/sites/dell/2011/12/20/the-history-and-future-of-cloud-computing/*) like J.C.R. Licklider—who thought computing resources would become a public utility like electricity-—it has only been recently with the start of AWS in 2006 (*http://www.zdnet.com/how-amazon-exposed-its-guts-the-history-of-awss-ec2-3040155310/*) and Windows Azure in 2008 (*http://news.cnet.com/microsoft-launches-windows-azure/*) that we have seen businesses seriously moving many of their core services outside of private data centers. There have been many discussions and descriptions about what cloud computing is and its value to businesses. However, in general we characterize it as a set of computing resources, CPU, memory, disk, and the like that is available to an end user and the interactions that user has with these resources.

AWS Service Delivery Models

There are a number of delivery models for cloud services and how the end user accesses these resources in the cloud. We will focus on the delivery methods specific to AWS and the resources used in this book for Elastic MapReduce.

Platform as a Service

Platform as a Service (PaaS) allows the deployment of custom-built applications within the cloud provider's infrastructure. Elastic MapReduce is an example of an Amazon cloud service that is delivered as a PaaS. As a user, you can deploy a number of preconfigured Amazon EC2 instances with the EMR software preinstalled. You can specify the compute capacity and memory for these instances, and have access to make configuration changes to the EMR software. Amazon takes care of much of the customization needed for the EMR software to work in its data center and with other Amazon services.

As a user of EMR, you can tune the configuration to your application's needs and install much of application through Amazon's APIs and tools.

Infrastructure as a Service

Infrastructure as a Service (IaaS) is probably the simplest cloud delivery method, and one that seems most familiar to many professionals that have developed solutions to run in private data centers. As a consumer of IaaS services, you have access to computing resources of CPU, memory, disk, network, and other resources. Amazon's EC2 is an example of a cloud service delivered in the IaaS model. You can specify the size of an EC2 instance and the operating system used, but it is up to you as a consumer of an EC2 instance to install OS patches, configure OS settings, and install third-party applications and software components.

Storage as a Service

Storage as a Service (SaaS) allows you to store files or data in the provider's data center. Amazon S3 and Amazon Glacier are the storage services we use throughout this book. Amazon charges on a per-gigabyte basis for these services and has replication and durability options.

We have discussed some of the benefits of AWS throughout the book, but we would be remiss if we did not cover many of the key issues businesses must consider when moving critical business data and infrastructure into the cloud.

Performance

Performance in cloud computing can vary widely between cloud providers. This variability can be due to the time of day, applications running, and how many customers have signed up for service from the cloud provider. It is a result of how the physical hardware of memory and CPU in a cloud provider is shared among all the customers.

Most cloud providers operate in a multitenancy model where a single physical server may run many instances of virtual computers. Each virtual instance uses some amount of memory and CPU from the physical server on which it resides. The sharing and allocation of the physical resources of a server to each virtual instance is the job of a piece of software installed by the cloud provider called the *hypervisor*. Amazon uses a highly customized version of the Xen hypervisor for AWS (*http://aws.amazon.com/ articles/1697*). As a user of EC2 and other AWS services, you may have your EC2 instance running on the same physical hardware as many other Amazon EC2 customers.

Let's look at a number of scenarios at a cloud provider to understand why variability in performance can occur. Let's assume we have three physical servers, each with four virtual instances running. Figure B-1 shows a number of virtual instances running in a cloud provider.

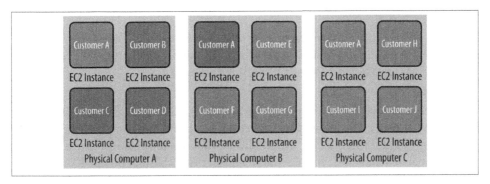

Figure B-1. Physical servers in the cloud with no hypervisor vacancies

Multiple customers are running on the same physical server and kept separated virtually by the hypervisor. In Figure B-1, Physical Computer A has four virtual instances running with Customer B, C, and D running at 100% utilization. Physical Computer B does not have the same load profile with only one instance, Customer A, running an instance at 100% utilization. Physical Computer C does not have any instances with high resource utilization and all instances on this computer are running at 25% or less utilization. Even though Customer A has virtual instances running at low utilization on server A and server C in this scenario, the software running on server A may run noticeably slower than the software on server C due to the high load placed on the server by other virtual instances running on the same physical hardware. This issue is commonly referred to as the "noisy neighbor" problem.

We know that cloud providers rarely run at 100% utilization and due to the elasticity provided in cloud infrastructure, vacancies on an individual server would occur from time to time. Figure B-2 shows the same physical servers at a later time.

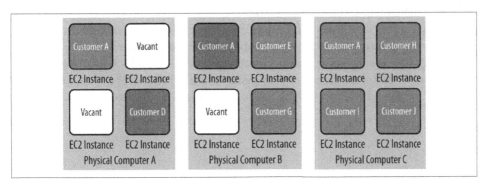

Figure B-2. Physical servers in the cloud with three hypervisor vacancies

Now a number of vacancies have appeared due to some customers turning off excess capacity. The software on server A may now be performing significantly better and may be similar to the performance of server C because server A now has a 50% vacancy in its hypervisor.

This is an initial shock to many businesses that first move to the cloud when they are accustomed to dedicated physical servers for applications. AWS provides a number of ways to tailor cloud services to meet performance needs.

Auto scaling

Amazon allows you to quickly scale up and down additional instances of many of its AWS services. This allows you to meet variable traffic and compute needs quickly and only pay for what you use. In a traditional data center, business have to estimate potential demand, and typically find themselves purchasing too much or too little capacity.

Multiple EC2 configuration options

Amazon has a wide variety of configurations for EC2 instances. They range from micro instances all the way up to double extra-large instances. Each of the instance types has a defined allocation of memory and CPU capacity. Amazon lists compute capacity in terms of EC2 compute capacity. This is a rough measure of the CPU performance of an early 2006 1.7 GHz Xeon processor and allows businesses to translate current physical hardware requirements to cloud performance. Elastic MapReduce uses these EC2 instance types to execute MapReduce jobs. You can find more information on Amazon EC2 instance types on the AWS website under Amazon EC2 Instance Types (*http://aws.amazon.com/ec2/instance-types/*).

EC2 dedicated instances

Businesses may have very specialized needs for which they would like greater control over the variable aspects of cloud computing, Amazon offers EC2 dedicated instances as an option for customers with these needs. An EC2 dedicated instance includes Amazon EC2 instances that run on hardware dedicated to a single customer. This is similar to the traditional data center hosting model where customers have their own dedicated hardware that only runs their software. A key difference, though, is that customers still only pay for the services they use and can scale up and down these dedicated resources as needed. However, there is an extra per-hour cost for this service that can greatly increase the cost of cloud services. You can find more information on dedicated EC2 instances on the AWS website under Amazon EC2 Dedicated Instances (*http://aws.amazon.com/dedicated-instances/*).

Provisioned IOPS

Some applications require a high amount of disk read and write capacity. This is typically measured as inputs and outputs per second (IOPS). Database systems and other specialized applications are typically more bound by IOPS performance than CPU and memory. Amazon has recently added the ability to specify IOPS capacity and needs to its AWS EC2 instances.

We explored the performance of Elastic MapReduce throughout this book and helped you understand how to size your AWS capacity. Chapter 6, in particular, looked at the costs and trade-offs of different AWS options for our Elastic MapReduce application.

Elasticity and Growth

IT elasticity and the ability to quickly scale up and scale down is a major reason why many enterprises begin to look at moving resources to the cloud. In the traditional IT model, operations and engineering management need to evaluate what they believe will be expected demand, and scale up IT infrastructure many months before the launch of a project or a major initiative. Throughout the lifetime of an application there is an ongoing cycle of estimating future IT resource demand with actual application demand growth. This typically creates periods of excess and undercapacity throughout the lifetime of an application due to the time between demand estimation and bringing new capacity online in the data center.

AWS and cloud services reduce the time between increased demand for services and capacity being available to meet that demand. Amazon Elastic MapReduce allows you to scale capacity in the following ways.

Fixed Capacity

You can specify the size and number of each of the EC2 instances used in your EMR Job Flows by specifying the instance count for each of the EMR Job Flow components. Figure B-3 shows an example of the New Cluster, or Job Flow, configuration screen where the number of EC2 instances are specified.

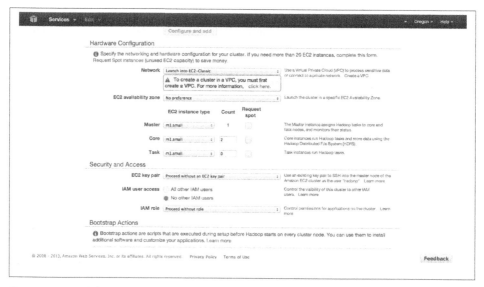

Figure B-3. Configuring compute capacity for an Amazon EMR Job Flow

The size and number of instances will affect the amount of data you can process over time. This is the capacity the job flow will use throughout its lifetime, but can be adjusted using Amazon's command-line tools or EMR Console to increase the instance counts while the job is running. You will be charged reserve or on-demand hourly rates unless you choose to request spot instances.

Variable Capacity

Amazon offers spot instance capacity for a number of the AWS services. Spot instances allow customers to bid for spare compute capacity by naming the price they are willing to pay for additional capacity. When the bid price exceeds the current spot price, the additional EC2 instances are launched. Figure B-4 shows an example of bidding for spot capacity for an EMR Job Flow.

We explored spot capacity in greater detail in Chapter 6, where we reviewed the cost analysis of EMR configurations.

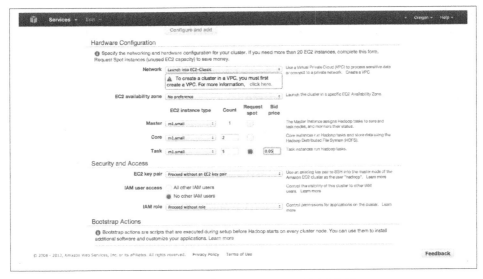

Figure B-4. Bidding for spot capacity for an Amazon EMR Job Flow

Security

Concern about security is one of the biggest inhibitors to using cloud services in most organizations. According to a 2009 Forrester survey of North American and European businesses, 50% said their chief reason for avoiding cloud computing was security concerns. Within five years, however, Forrester expects cloud security (*http://www.infor mationweek.com/security/management/cloud-security-to-reap-15-billion-by-201/227900576*) to be one of the primary drivers for *adopting* cloud computing.

So why has there been such a change in the view of security in the cloud? A lot of this has come from the cloud providers themselves realizing that a key to increasing cloud adoption is a focus on security. IBM (*http://www-03.ibm.com/security/cloud-security.html*) and Amazon AWS (*http://aws.amazon.com/security/*) have come out in recent years with a robust set of details on how they protect cloud services and the results of independent evaluations of their security and responses to independent organizations like the Cloud Security Alliance (*http://bit.ly/1d1OysH*).

Security Is a Shared Responsibility

Amazon has an impressive set of compliance and security credentials on its AWS Security and Compliance Center (*http://aws.amazon.com/security/*). Delving deeper into the AWS security whitepapers (*http://media.amazonwebservices.com/pdf/AWS_Securi ty_Whitepaper.pdf*), clients will note that Amazon has clearly stated that security is a shared responsibility in AWS. Amazon certifies the infrastructure, physical security, and host operating system. This takes a significant portion of the burden of maintaining compliance and security off of AWS customers. However, AWS customers are still responsible for patching the software they install into the infrastructure, guest operating system updates, and firewall and access policies in AWS. AWS customers will need to evaluate their in-house policies and how they translate to cloud services.

Data Security in Elastic MapReduce

Amazon EMR heavily uses S3 for data input and output with Job Flows. All data transfers to and from S3 are performed via SSL. Also, the data read and written by EMR is subject to the permissions set on the data in the form of access control lists (ACLs). An EMR job only has access to the data written by the same user. You can control these permissions by editing the S3 bucket's permissions (*http://docs.aws.amazon.com/AmazonS3/ latest/UG/EditingBucketPermissions.html*) to allow only the applications that need access to the data to use it.

 Amazon has a number of excellent whitepapers at its Security and Compliance Center (*http://aws.amazon.com/security*). A review of its security overview (*http://media.amazonwebservices.com/pdf/ AWS_Security_Whitepaper.pdf*) with your internal security team should be done before you move critical components and data to AWS services. Every project should also review the list of security best practices (*http://media.amazonwebservices.com/Whitepaper_Securi ty_Best_Practices_2010.pdf*) prior to launch to verify it is compliant with Amazon's recommendations. If your organization works with medical and patient data, make sure to also check out the AWS HIPAA and HITECH compliance whitepapers (*http://media.amazonweb services.com/AWS_HIPAA_Whitepaper_Final.pdf*).

Uptime and Availability

As applications and services are moved to the cloud, businesses need to evaluate and determine the risk of having an outage of their cloud services. This is a concern even with private data centers, but many organizations fear a lack of control when they no longer have physical access to their data center resources. For some, this fear has been validated by a number of high-profile outages and cloud service providers, including Amazon AWS services. The most recent was the infamous Christmas Eve AWS outage (*http://aws.amazon.com/message/680587/*) that took Netflix services offline during the holiday season.

AWS has a number of resources to help customers manage availability and uptime risks to their cloud services.

Regions and availability zones

Amazon has data centers located in the United States and around the globe. These locations are detailed as regions, and customers can pick multiple regions when setting up AWS services to reduce the risk of an outage in an Amazon region. Each region has redundancy built in, with multiple data centers laid out in each region in what Amazon calls availability zones. Amazon's architecture center (*http://aws.amazon.com/architecture/*) details how to make use of these features to build fault-tolerant applications on the AWS platform.

Service level agreement (SLA)

Amazon provides uptime guarantees for a number of the AWS services we covered in this book. These SLAs provide for 99.95% uptime and availability (*http://aws.amazon.com/ec2-sla/*) for the EC2 instances, and 99.9% availability for S3 (*http://aws.amazon.com/s3-sla/*) data services. Businesses are eligible for service credits of up to 25% when availability drops below certain availability thresholds.

Installation and Setup

The application built throughout this book makes use of the open source software Java, Hadoop, Pig, and Hive. Many of these software components are preinstalled and configured in Amazon EMR as well as the other AWS services used in examples. However, to build and test many of the examples in this book, you many find it easier or more in line with your own organizational policies to install these components locally. For the Java MapReduce jobs, you will be required to install Java locally to develop the Map-Reduce application.

This appendix covers the installation and setup of these software components to help prepare you for developing the components covered in the book.

Prerequisites

Many of the book's examples (and Hadoop itself) are written in Java. To use Hadoop and build the examples in this book, you will need to have Java installed. The examples in this book were built using the Oracle Java Development Kit (*http://www.oracle.com/technetwork/java/javase/downloads/index.html*). There are now many variations of the Java JDK available from OpenJDK to GNU Java. The code examples may work with these, but the Oracle JDK is still widely available, free, and the most widely used due to the long history of development of Java under Sun prior to Oracle purchasing the rights to Java. Depending on the Job Flow type you are creating and which packages you want to install locally, you may need multiple versions of Java installed. Also, a local installation of Pig and Hadoop will require Java v1.6 or greater.

Hadoop and many of the scripts and examples in this book were developed on a Linux/Unix-based system. Development and work can be done under Windows, but you should install Cygwin (*http://www.cygwin.com/*) to support the scripting examples in this book. When installing Cygwin, make sure to select the Bash shell and OpenSSL features to be able to develop and run the MapReduce examples locally on Windows systems.

 Hadoop, Hive, and Pig require the JAVA_HOME environment variable to be set. It is also typically good practice to have Java in the PATH so scripts and applications can easily find it. On a Linux machine, you can use the following command to specify these settings:

```
export JAVA_HOME=/usr/java/latest
export PATH=$PATH:$JAVA_HOME/bin
```

Installing Hadoop

The MapReduce framework used in Amazon EMR is a core technology stack that is part of Hadoop. In many of the examples in this book, the application was built locally and tested in Hadoop before it was uploaded into Amazon EMR.

Even if you do not intend to run Hadoop locally, many of the Java libraries needed to build the examples are included as part of the Hadoop distribution from Apache. The local installation of Hadoop also allowed us to run and debug the applications prior to loading them into Amazon EMR and incurring runtime charges testing them out. Hadoop can be downloaded directly from the Apache Hadoop website (*http://hadoop.apache.org/releases.html*).

In writing this book, we chose to use Hadoop version 0.20.205.0. This version is one of the supported Amazon EMR Hadoop versions, but is currently in the Hadoop download archive. Amazon regularly updates Hadoop and many of the other open source tools used in AWS. If your project requires a different version of Hadoop, refer to Amazon's EMR developer documentation (*http://docs.aws.amazon.com/ElasticMapReduce/latest/DeveloperGuide/emr-plan-hadoop-version.html*) for the versions that are supported.

After you install Hadoop, it is convenient to add Hadoop to the path and define a variable that references the location of Hadoop for other scripts and routines that use it. The following example shows these variables being added to the .bash_profile on a Linux system to define the home location and add Hadoop to the path:

```
$ export HADOOP_INSTALL=/home/user/hadoop-0.20.205.0
$ export PATH=$PATH:$HADOOP_INSTALL/bin
```

You can confirm the installation and setup of Hadoop by running it at the command line. The following example shows running the hadoop command line and the version installed:

```
$ hadoop version
Hadoop 0.20.205.0
```

```
Subversion https://svn.apache.org/repos/asf/hadoop/
common/branches/branch-0.20-security-205 -r 1179940
Compiled by hortonfo on Fri Oct  7 06:26:14 UTC 2011
$
```

 Hadoop can be configured to run in a standalone, pseudodistributed, or distributed mode. The default mode is standalone. In standalone mode, everything runs inside a single JVM, and this mode is most suitable for debugging and testing MapReduce jobs. The other Hadoop modes are suited to building out a true Hadoop cluster with multiple servers acting as Hadoop nodes. Because this book is about using Amazon EMR as your Hadoop cluster, we assume you will be using Hadoop only for MapReduce development and testing. If you would like to build out a more full-blown Hadoop cluster, O'Reilly has a great book on Hadoop, *Hadoop: The Definitive Guide, 3E*, by Tom White.

Hadoop has a fairly aggressive release cycle of close to 24 releases in 18 months. Amazon does not update Amazon EMR as aggressively, so always review Amazon's supported Hadoop version when starting new projects!

Building MapReduce Applications

The majority of the code samples and applications built in this book are written in Java. Most Java developers today use a Java IDE to develop Java applications. The most popular Java IDEs available today are Eclipse (*http://www.eclipse.org/downloads/*), Net-Beans (*https://netbeans.org/*), and IntelliJ (*http://www.jetbrains.com/idea/*). Each of these IDEs has its strengths and weaknesses, but any of these environments can be used to build and develop the Java MapReduce applications in this book.

We used the Eclipse Java IDE and installed the Eclipse Maven plug-in, m2eclipse (*http://eclipse.org/m2e/download/*), to manage application dependencies. You can install the m2eclipse plug-in through the Install New Software option inside of Eclipse.

To include the dependencies needed to build the MapReduce applications, create a Maven project inside of Eclipse by selecting File→New→Other. The Maven project option should be available after you install the m2eclipse plug-in. Figure C-1 shows the Maven New Project option in Eclipse.

Figure C-1. Creating an Eclipse Maven project

Select the program and project name of your application when going through the Eclipse New Project Wizard. After the project is created, the Hadoop dependencies will need to be added to the project so the application can make use of the Hadoop base classes, types, and methods. You can add the Hadoop core dependencies by selecting the *pom.xml* file that is in the root of the project. The *pom.xml* lists the Maven project details and the dependencies of the project. After opening the *pom.xml* file in Eclipse, click on the Dependencies tab to add new dependencies. The Hadoop core JAR files can be searched for and added to the project as shown in Figure C-2.

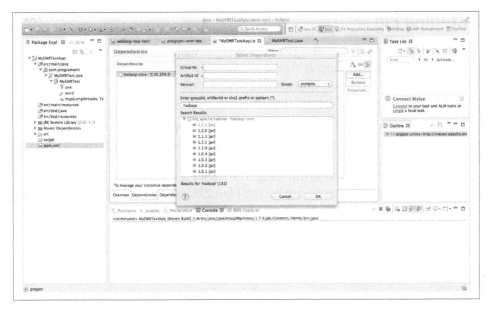

Figure C-2. Adding Hadoop dependencies in Eclipse

Running MapReduce Applications Locally

With Hadoop installed locally, you can build and test your MapReduce application locally before uploading to Amazon EMR. The parameters and settings to the hadoop command-line should look very similar to the parameters passed to Amazon EMR. To test locally, run the hadoop command line application by telling it to execute the MapReduce JAR with the driver class and specified input and output locations. The following shows an example local run of an application:

```
$ hadoop jar MyEMRApp.jar \
    com.programemr.MyEMRAppDriver \
    NASA_access_log_Jul95 \
    ~/output
13/10/13 22:02:04 WARN util.NativeCodeLoader: Unable to load native-hadoop ...
13/10/13 22:02:04 INFO mapred.FileInputFormat: Total input paths to process : 1
13/10/13 22:02:04 INFO mapred.JobClient: Running job: job_local_0001
13/10/13 22:02:04 INFO mapred.Task:  Using ResourceCalculatorPlugin : null
13/10/13 22:02:04 INFO mapred.MapTask: numReduceTasks: 1
13/10/13 22:02:04 INFO mapred.MapTask: io.sort.mb = 100
13/10/13 22:02:04 INFO mapred.MapTask: data buffer = 79691776/99614720
13/10/13 22:02:04 INFO mapred.MapTask: record buffer = 262144/327680
13/10/13 22:02:05 INFO mapred.JobClient:  map 0% reduce 0%
13/10/13 22:02:06 INFO mapred.MapTask: Starting flush of map output
...
```

Installing Pig

In Chapter 4, we explored utilizing Apache Pig to develop Job Flows for Amazon EMR. We developed and tested many of the Pig scripts used in this book utilizing an interactive Pig session hosted at Amazon. This allows you to directly interact with an Amazon EMR cluster with Hadoop and Pig preconfigured and installed for you.

Many organizations, however, may not want to do development on a live cluster or incur the AWS charges for development and testing efforts. Just like Hadoop, Apache Pig can be downloaded and installed locally. Hadoop and Java are prerequisites for Pig, and you will need to install them prior to using Pig. The latest Pig version supported by Amazon EMR (*http://docs.aws.amazon.com/ElasticMapReduce/latest/DeveloperGuide/ Pig_SupportedVersions.html*) at the time of this writing was v0.11.1. You can download Apache Pig directly from the Apache Pig website (*http://pig.apache.org/*).

After you install Pig, run `pig` at the command line to confirm the installation and execution of Pig:

```
$ ./pig
2013-10-14 21:52:53,964 [main] INFO  org.apache.pig.Main -
Apache Pig version 0.11.1 (r1459641) compiled Mar 22 2013, 02:13:53
2013-10-14 21:52:53,964 [main] INFO  org.apache.pig.Main -
Logging error messages to: /Users/piguser/devtools/pig-0.11.1/
bin/pig_1381801973961.log
2013-10-14 21:52:53,982 [main] INFO  org.apache.pig.impl.util.Utils -
Default bootup file /Users/user/.pigbootup not found
2013-10-14 21:52:54,153 [main] INFO  org.apache.pig.backend.hadoop.
executionengine.HExecutionEngine - Connecting to hadoop file
system at: file:///
2013-10-14 21:52:54.219 java[2611:1703] Unable to load realm info
from SCDynamicStore
grunt>
```

Installing Hive

As with Pig, the easiest way to get Hive and Hadoop up and running and configured is utilizing an Amazon EMR interactive Job Flow. Creating an interactive session in Amazon EMR is covered in Chapter 4. However, if you need to install Hive, you can download it from the Apache Hive website (*http://hive.apache.org/*).

After installing Hive, it is convenient to add Hive to the path and define a variable that references the location of Hive for other scripts. The following example shows these variables being added to the `.bash_profile` on a Linux system to define the home location and add Hive to the path:

```
$ export HIVE_HOME=/home/user/hive-0.11.0
$ export PATH=$PATH:$HADOOP_INSTALL/bin:$HIVE_HOME/bin
```

Just like with Pig, you can confirm the installation and setup of Hive by running it at the command line:

```
$ hive

Logging initialized using configuration in jar:file:/Users/user/devtools/
hive-0.11.0/lib/hive-common-0.11.0.jar!/hive-log4j.properties
Hive history file=/tmp/user/hive_job_log_user_6659@localhost.
local_201310201926_1381209376.txt
2013-10-20 19:26:12.324 java[6659:1703] Unable to load realm info
from SCDynamicStore
hive>
```

 Hive is very dependent on the version of Hadoop installed, and the project does not keep many of the previous archived versions of Hive that are needed for the earlier versions of Hadoop. Though the Apache Hive website (*http://hive.apache.org/releases.html*) notes that the latest versions of Hive are compatible with Hadoop version 0.20.205.0, running Hive against this version results in an ALLOW_UNQUOTED_CON TROL_CHARS error. If you need to run Hive locally for your project, we recommend running Hadoop v1.0.3, which is also a version of Hadoop currently available in Amazon EMR.

Index

We'd like to hear your suggestions for improving our indexes. Send email to index@oreilly.com.

About the Authors

Kevin J. Schmidt is a senior manager at Dell SecureWorks, Inc., an industry-leading MSSP, which is part of Dell. He is responsible for the design and development of a major part of the company's SIEM platform. This includes data acquisition, correlation, and analysis of log data. Prior to SecureWorks, Kevin worked for Reflex Security, where he worked on an IPS engine and antivirus software. And prior to this, he was a lead developer and architect at GuardedNet, Inc., which built one of the industry's first SIEM platforms. He is also a commissioned officer in the United States Navy Reserve (USNR). He has more than 19 years of experience in software development and design, 11 of which have been in the network security space. He holds a BS in computer science. Kevin has spent time designing cloud service components at Dell, including virtualized components to run in Dell's own cloud. These components are used to protect customers who use Dell's cloud infrastructure. Additionally, he has been working with Hadoop, machine learning, and other technologies in the cloud. Kevin is coauthor of *Essential SNMP, 2E* (O'Reilly) and *Logging and Log Management* (Syngress).

Christopher Phillips is a manager and senior software developer at Dell SecureWorks, Inc., an industry-leading MSSP, which is part of Dell. He is responsible for the design and development of the company's Threat Intelligence service platform. He is also responsible for a team involved in integrating log and event information from many third-party providers that allow customers to have all of their core security information delivered to and analyzed by the Dell SecureWorks systems and security professionals. Prior to Dell SecureWorks, Chris worked for McKesson and Allscripts, where he worked with clients on HIPAA compliance, security, and healthcare systems integration. He has more than 18 years of experience in software development and design. He holds a BS in computer science and an MBA. Chris has spent time designing and developing virtualization and cloud Infrastructure as a Service strategies at Dell to help its security services scale globally. Additionally, he has been working with Hadoop, Pig scripting languages, and Amazon Elastic MapReduce to develop strategies to gain insights and analyze Big Data issues in the cloud. Chris is coauthor of *Logging and Log Management* (Syngress).

Colophon

The animal on the cover of *Programming Elastic MapReduce* is the eastern kingsnake (*lampropeltis getula getula*). The eastern kingsnake is a subspecies of the common kingsnake (*Lampropeltis getula*) that mostly lives in the Eastern United States. Common kingsnakes can be found in swamps, streams, grasslands, and deserts across the United States and Mexico.

Adult common kingsnakes, depending on the subspecies, are 20 to 78 inches in length and weigh between .62 and 5 pounds. They can be black, blue-black, or dark brown colored with two to four dozen white rings around their body. Even though they eat lizards, rodents, and birds, they also frequently eat other snakes. They eat other snakes by biting the mouth of their prey and stoping it from being able to counterattack. Common kingsnakes are also immune to the venom of other snakes. They have no venom themselves, however, and are considered harmless to humans.

There are eight subspecies of common kingsnake, which may be the reason why this species is known by several dozen names. Depending on the location, the common kingsnake is called the Carolina Kingsnake, North American king snake, oakleaf rattler, thunder snake, black moccasin, thunderbolt, wamper, master snake, and pine snake.

The cover image is from *Wood's Animate Creation*. The cover fonts are URW Typewriter and Guardian Sans. The text font is Adobe Minion Pro; the heading font is Adobe Myriad Condensed; and the code font is Dalton Maag's Ubuntu Mono.

Get even more for your money.

Join the O'Reilly Community, and register the O'Reilly books you own. It's free, and you'll get:

- $4.99 ebook upgrade offer
- 40% upgrade offer on O'Reilly print books
- Membership discounts on books and events
- Free lifetime updates to ebooks and videos
- Multiple ebook formats, DRM FREE
- Participation in the O'Reilly community
- Newsletters
- Account management
- 100% Satisfaction Guarantee

Signing up is easy:

1. **Go to: oreilly.com/go/register**
2. **Create an O'Reilly login.**
3. **Provide your address.**
4. **Register your books.**

Note: English-language books only

To order books online:
oreilly.com/store

For questions about products or an order:
orders@oreilly.com

To sign up to get topic-specific email announcements and/or news about upcoming books, conferences, special offers, and new technologies:
elists@oreilly.com

For technical questions about book content:
booktech@oreilly.com

To submit new book proposals to our editors:
proposals@oreilly.com

O'Reilly books are available in multiple DRM-free ebook formats. For more information:
oreilly.com/ebooks

Spreading the knowledge of innovators   oreilly.com

Have it your way.

O'Reilly eBooks

- Lifetime access to the book when you buy through oreilly.com
- Provided in up to four DRM-free file formats, for use on the devices of your choice: PDF, .epub, Kindle-compatible .mobi, and Android .apk
- Fully searchable, with copy-and-paste and print functionality
- Alerts when files are updated with corrections and additions

oreilly.com/ebooks/

Safari Books Online

- Access the contents and quickly search over 7000 books on technology, business, and certification guides
- Learn from expert video tutorials, and explore thousands of hours of video on technology and design topics
- Download whole books or chapters in PDF format, at no extra cost, to print or read on the go
- Get early access to books as they're being written
- Interact directly with authors of upcoming books
- Save up to 35% on O'Reilly print books

See the complete Safari Library at safari.oreilly.com

O'REILLY®

CPSIA information can be obtained at www.ICGtesting.com
Printed in the USA
BVOW10s1325141213

339053BV00002B/2/P

9 781449 363628